Anonymous

Church Song

A repertory of music for the rendering of the responses, canticles, Psalms

Anonymous

Church Song
A repertory of music for the rendering of the responses, canticles, Psalms

ISBN/EAN: 9783337038557

Printed in Europe, USA, Canada, Australia, Japan

Cover: Foto ©Lupo / pixelio.de

More available books at **www.hansebooks.com**

---:o:---

A REPERTORY OF MUSIC

FOR THE RENDERING OF THE

RESPONSES, CANTICLES, PSALMS & HYMNALS

OF THE

Evangelical Lutheran Church.

BY

JOSEPH A. SEISS, D. D.,

Pastor of the Church of the Holy Communion, Philadelphia,

AND

CHARLES PILLING ENGELMANN.

NEW AND ENLARGED EDITION.

PHILADELPHIA:
LUTHERAN BOOK STORE.
1889.

PREFACE.

---o---

Though prepared to meet local necessities, this Book has met with so much favor as to exhaust previous issues and to call for another edition. In sending it once more to press, the opportunity has been embraced to revise and enlarge it, and thus to adapt it to a more general use. A new form for Morning Service, a third *Gloria in Excelsis*, a new *Sanctus*, and an Appendix of 44 popular Metrical Tunes, have been added to this edition. The Music throughout, in addition to what has been written expressly for this Book, has been selected with much care, from all sources, ancient and modern, classic and popular, in order to furnish ample materials for the appropriate and easy rendering of all parts of the worship prescribed in the various English Liturgies and Hymnals of the Evangelical Lutheran Church. The publication is mainly a matter of love, as many editions will need to be sold before the cost of its production can be reimbursed. But the department to which it is a contribution is so important, that it is thought worth while to make sacrifices to supply it well. May the Divine blessing accompany this effort to advance pure and worthy song in the house and worship of the Lord, and help His people to praise Him as becometh His excellency!

NOTE.—The musical markings will be readily understood by every musician. The two dots (..), or the hyphen (-), indicate that the syllable preceding is to be held a little longer by way of emphasis. A particular beauty will be added by an observance of these marks. In the Psalms and Canticles, the words forming the cadences are printed in heavier type, that the eye may the more readily distinguish them from the recitative portions. The only general direction to be given is, to be careful not to render too slowly, which is the common fault, but with activity and animation. It is also very desirable that, in rendering the Hymns, all interludes between the verses should be abandoned as a tiresome, uncouth, and meaningless fashion. A pause, the length of a single bar, is in far better taste, and ample for the transition from one stanza to another.

CONTENTS.

I. THE MORNING SERVICE.   PAGE
   1. First Form 5–18
   2. Second Form 19–24

II. THE HOLY COMMUNION.
   1. First Form 25–32
   2. Second Form 33–38

III. EVENING SERVICE............................. 39–46

IV. THE LITANY AND SUFFRAGES.................. 47–57

V. THE CANTICLES.............................. 58–61

VI. THE PSALMS................................ 62–85

VII. METRICAL TUNES............................ 89–206

VIII. APPENDIX OF METRICAL TUNES................ 207–231

IX. INDEXES.
   1. Alphabetical Index of Tunes, including Appendix... 232–234
   2. Metrical Index, not including Appendix............ 235–237
   3. Index of Appendix, Tunes and Metres............... 238

X. CHORISTER'S REGISTERS, not including Appendix.
   1. For Book of Worship, (South.)..................... 239–243
   2. " Book of Worship, (North.). 244–249
   3. " Church Book, (General Council.)................. 250–255

CHURCH SONG.

MORNING SERVICE.

Min. IN THE NAME OF THE FATHER, AND OF THE SON, AND OF THE HOLY GHOST.

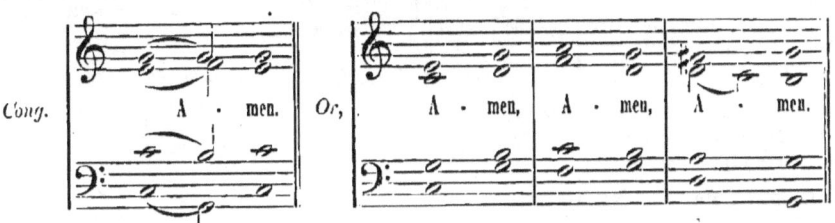

Min. Beloved in the Lord! etc.   Our help is in the Name of the Lord.

Min. I said, I will confess my transgressions unto the Lord.

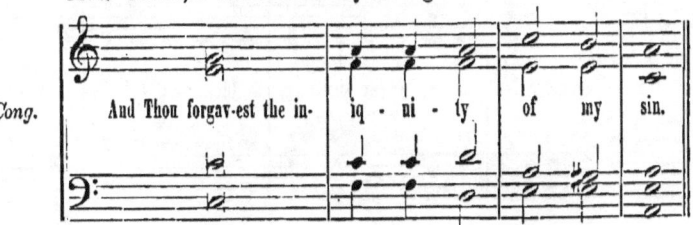

The Confession of Sin.

Min. ALMIGHTY GOD, our Maker and Redeemer, we poor sinners confess unto Thee, etc. *Ending: to the end that by Thy grace we may come to everlasting life, through Jesus Christ our Lord.*

MORNING SERVICE.

¶ *Then the Minister, standing, shall pronounce*

The Absolution.

ALMIGHTY GOD, our heavenly Father, hath had mercy upon us, and for the sake of His dear Son, forgiveth us all our sins. To them that believe on His Name, He also giveth power to become the sons of God, and bestoweth upon them His Holy Spirit. He that believeth, and is baptized, shall be saved. Grant us, O Lord, this salvation.

A - men.

¶ *Then, all standing to the close of the* Collect, *shall be sung or said:*

The Introit.

¶ *The Introit appointed for the Day shall be used. It being said by the Minister, the* Gloria Patri *shall be sung or said by the Congregation.*

¶ *The Introit, except in the week before Easter, shall always end with the*

Gloria Patri.

GLORIA PATRI. No. I.

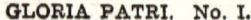

GLORIA PATRI. No. II.

MORNING SERVICE.

was in the be-gin-ning, is now, and ever shall be, world with-out end. A-men.

GLORIA PATRI. No. III. Chant No. I. From "Ein feste Burg," by LUTHER.

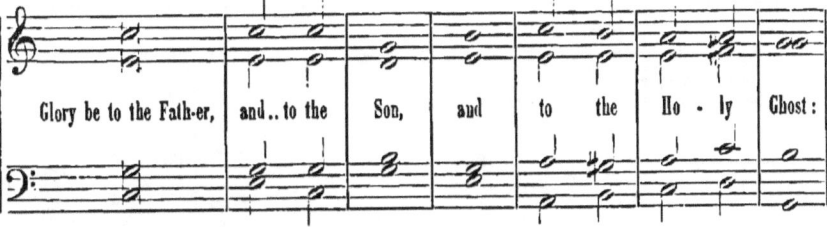

Glory be to the Fath-er, and .. to the Son, and to the Ho - ly Ghost:

As it was in the beginning, is now, and ever .. shall be, world with-out end. A - men.

¶ *Then shall follow the*

Kyrie.

¶ *The Kyrie may be said by the Minister, and sung or said after him by the Congregation, as here followeth; or it may be sung or said but once by the Minister and Congregation together.*

Min. Lord, have mer-cy upon us. | *Min.* Christ, have mer-cy upon us. | *Min.* Lord, have mercy upon us.

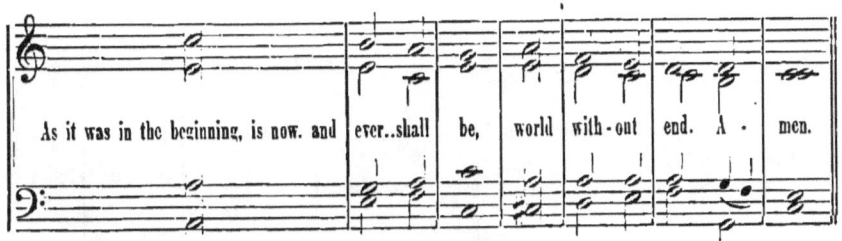

Lord, have mercy upon us.   Christ, have mercy upon us.   Lord, have mercy up - on us.
p   *mp*   *mf*

MORNING SERVICE.

¶ *Then shall be sung the Gloria in Excelsis, as here followeth; or instead of it may be sung the Te Deum Laudamus, or another Hymn of Praise.*

¶ *When the Te Deum is used, the Minister shall say,* We praise Thee, O God. *When the Gloria in Excelsis is used, he shall say:*

Glory be to God on high!

And the Congregation shall sing:

GLORIA IN EXCELSIS. No. I.

MORNING SERVICE.

℟ *Then shall the Minister say:*
The Lord be with you.
℟ *The Congregation shall sing:*

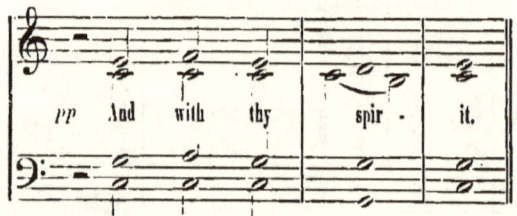

℟ *Then shall the Minister say the* Collect *appointed for the Day.*
℟ *The* Collect *ended, the Congregation shall sing:*

℟ *Then shall the Minister read the* Epistle *for the Day.*

The Epistle.

℟ *The* Epistle *ended, the Minister shall say:*
Here endeth the Epistle.

℟ *Then shall the* Hallelujah *be sung, except in the week before Easter.*

HALLELUJAH. No. I.   **HALLELUJAH. No. II.**

MORNING SERVICE.

HALLELUJAH. No. III.

¶ *Instead of the simple Hallelujah, a Sentence for the Season of the Church-Year may be sung with it; or a Psalm or Hymn may be sung after the Hallelujah.*

The Hallelujah and Sentence.

FOR THE ADVENT SEASON.

FOR THE EPIPHANY SEASON.

MORNING SERVICE.

FOR THE PASSION SEASON.

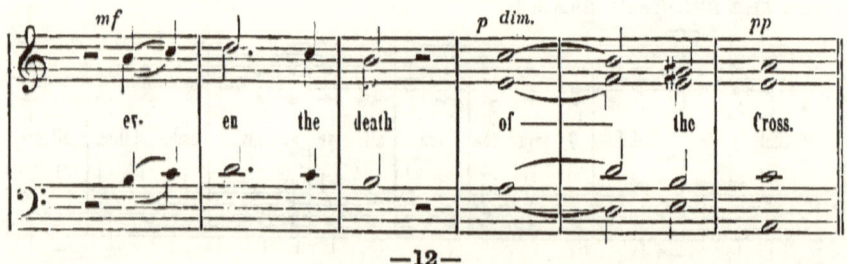

MORNING SERVICE.

FOR THE EASTER SEASON.

FOR THE SEASON OF PENTECOST.

MORNING SERVICE.

FOR THE SUNDAYS AFTER TRINITY.

Or this:

MORNING SERVICE.

¶ *Then shall the Minister announce the Gospel for the Day, saying:*

The Holy Gospel is written in the —— Chapter of St. ——, beginning at the —— Verse.

¶ *The Congregation may sing:*

GLORIA TIBI. No. I.   Or, GLORIA TIBI. No. II.

¶ *Then shall the Minister read:*

The Gospel for the Day.

¶ *The Gospel ended, the Minister shall say:* Here endeth the Gospel, *and the Congregation shall stand up, unless they have stood at the reading of the Gospel, and shall sing:*

LAUS TIBI. No. I.   Or, LAUS TIBI. No. II.

MORNING SERVICE.

❡ *Then shall the* Creed *be said or sung by the Minister and the Congregation. Either the Apostles' or the Nicene Creed may be used, but if there be a Communion, the Nicene Creed shall be used.*

The Apostles' Creed.

I believe in God, etc., | I believe in the Holy | Ghost; The Holy Christian | Church; The Communion of Saints; The Forgiveness of | sins; The Resurrection of the | body; | And the Life ev-er-last-ing. | A-men.

The Nicene Creed.

I believe in one God, etc., | And I believe in the Holy | Ghost. The Lord and Giver of | Life, Who proceedeth from the Father and the Son, Who with the Father and the Son to- | gether is worshipped and glo-ri- | fied, Who spake by the | prophets. And I believe one holy Christian and Apostolic

MORNING SERVICE.

¶ *Then shall the Minister announce the Hymn to be sung, and go into the pulpit. After the Hymn shall follow*

The Sermon.

¶ *When the Sermon is ended, the Congregation all standing up, and continuing to stand to the end of the* Lord's Prayer, *the Minister shall say:*

The peace of God, which passeth all understanding, keep your hearts and minds through Christ Jesus unto everlasting life.

¶ *Then shall the Congregation sing:*

CHANT. No. II.

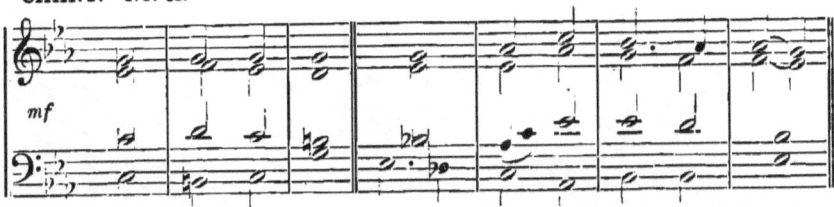

Or, CHANT. No. III.

CREATE in me a clean | heart, O | God : ‖
   And renew..a right | spirit..with- | in — | me.
Cast me not away | from Thy | presence : ‖
   And take not Thy | Holy | Spirit | from me.
Restore unto me the joy..of | Thy..sal- | vation : ‖
   And uphold..me | with — | Thy free | Spirit.

MORNING SERVICE.

¶ *Whilst this is sung, the Minister shall go to the Altar, and the singing ended, he shall offer prayer. He may use the Prayer given, or, if there be no Communion, the Litany, or the Suffrages, or a selection from the general and special Collects, or any other suitable prayer.*

The Prayer.

¶ *Then may the Minister make any needful announcements, and the Offerings of the Congregation be gathered. While the Offerings are being gathered, the Organist may play a voluntary, or the Choir sing some suitable sentence ending, upon the presentation of the Offerings, with*

and after that shall follow a Hymn *which shall end with a Doxology when there is no Communion. Whilst the Doxology is sung the Congregation shall stand.*

¶ *When the Doxology is ended, the Minister, standing before the Altar, shall pronounce*

The Benediction.

The Lord bless thee, and keep thee.
The Lord make His face shine upon thee, and be gracious unto thee.
The Lord lift up His countenance upon thee, and give thee peace.

¶ *The Congregation shall sing:*

MORNING SERVICE.
(*SECOND FORM.*)

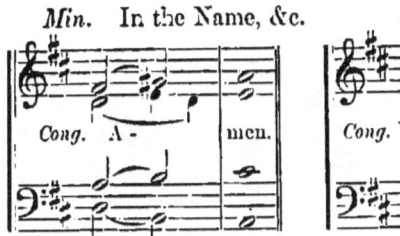

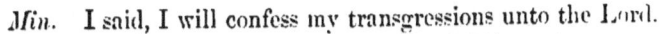

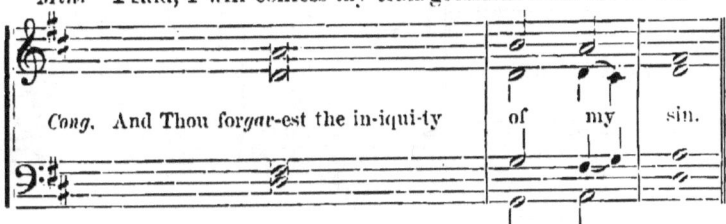

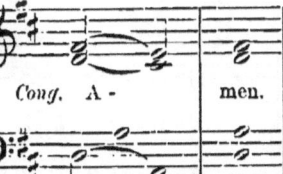
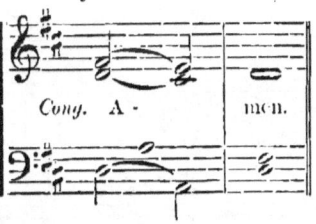

GLORIA PATRI. No. I.

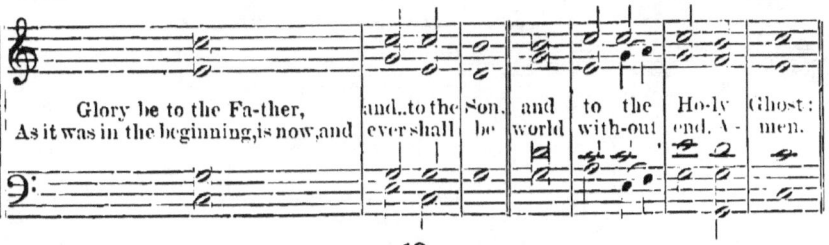

MORNING SERVICE.

GLORIA PATRI. No. II.
From N. Hermann, 1560.

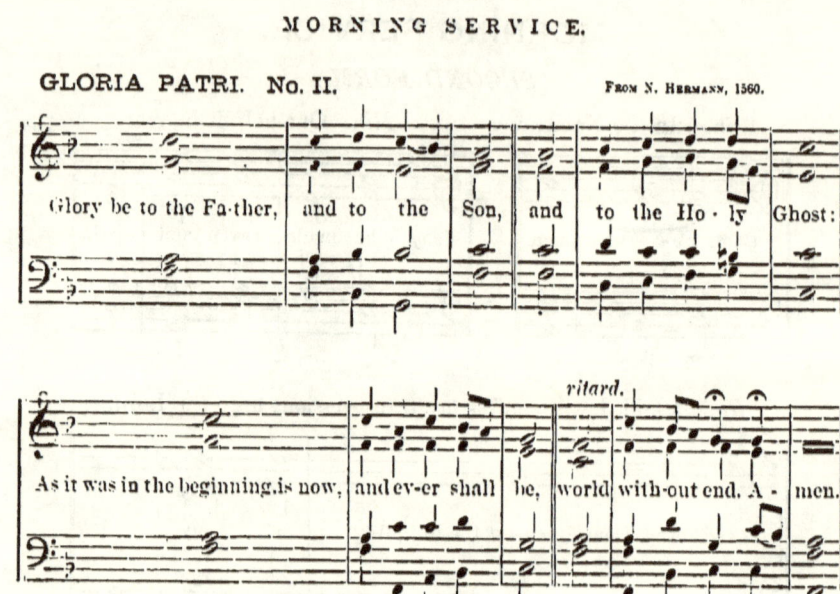

KYRIE.

MORNING SERVICE.

GLORIA IN EXCELSIS.

Min. Glory be to God on high.   CHARLES ZEUNER.

MORNING SERVICE.

THE SALUTATION.
I. *Min.* The Lord be with you. II.

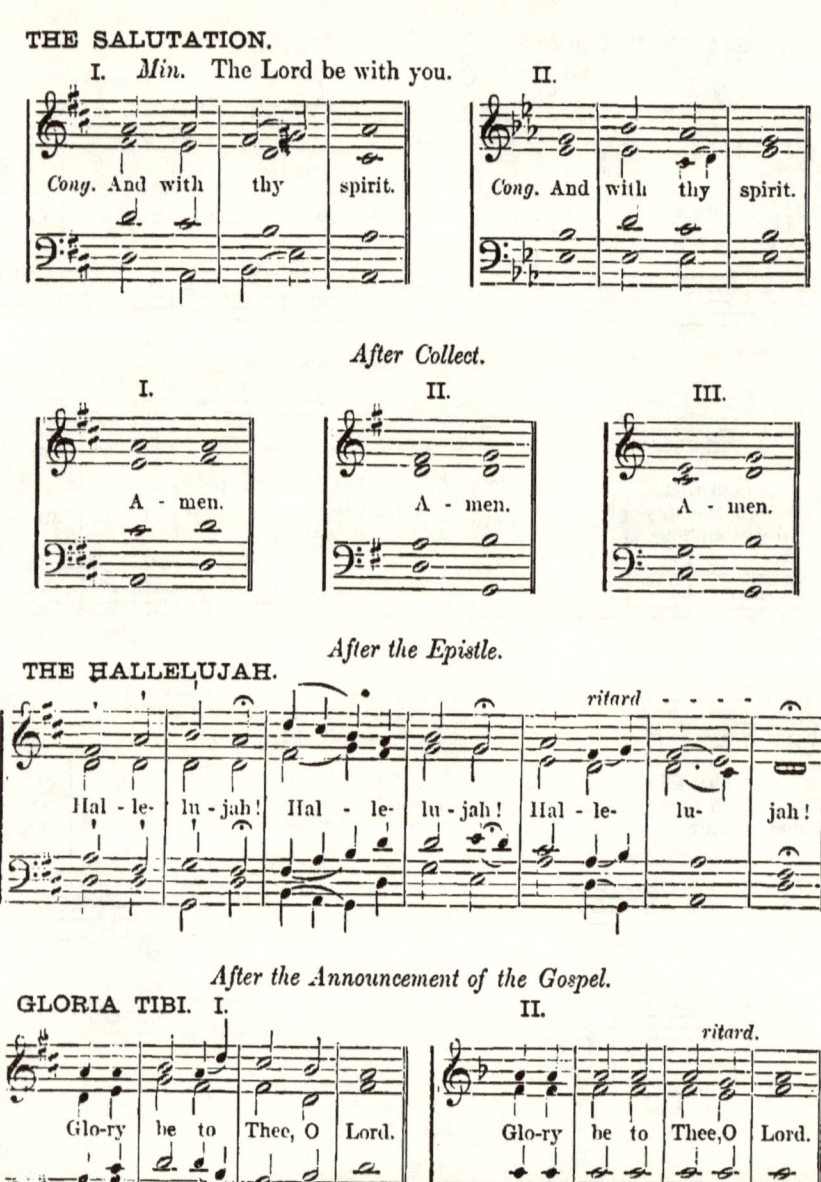

MORNING SERVICE.

At the end of the Reading of the Gospel.

After the Sermon.

CREATE in me a clean | heart, O | God : ‖
And renew..a right | spirit..with- | in— | me.
Cast me not away | from Thy | presence : ‖
And take not Thy | Holy | Spirit | from me.
Restore unto me the joy..of | Thy..sal- | vation : ‖
And uphold..me | with- | Thy free | Spirit.

After the Benediction.

O PARADISE.

Andante.   J. Barnby.

O Paradise! O Paradise! Who doth not crave for rest!
Who would not seek the happy land, Where they that loved are blest!
Where loyal hearts and true, Stand ever in the light,
All rapture through and through, In God's most holy sight.

O Paradise! O Paradise! I greatly long to see
That special place my dearest Lord In love prepares for me;
Where loyal hearts and true, Stand ever in the light,
All rapture through and through, In God's most holy sight.

Lord Jesus, King of Paradise, O keep me in Thy love,
And guide me to that happy land Of perfect rest above;
Where loyal hearts and true, Stand ever in the light,
All rapture through and through, In God's most holy sight.
                               AMEN.

The Holy Communion.

¶ *Whilst the Hymn after the General Prayer is sung, the Minister shall uncover the Communion vessels, and devoutly prepare for the administration of the* Holy Communion.

¶ *The Minister, standing before the Altar, shall begin the* Communion Service, *as here followeth, the Congregation all standing to the end of the* Agnus Dei.

Min. The Lord be with you.   *Min.* Lift up your hearts.

Min. Let us give thanks unto our Lord God.

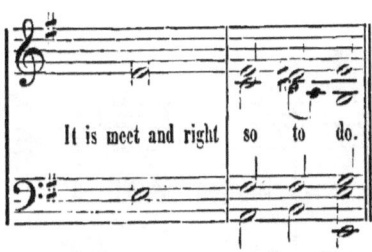

¶ *After the* Preface *shall follow immediately:*

Therefore with Angels and Archangels, and with all the company of heaven, we laud and magnify Thy glorious Name; evermore praising Thee, and saying:

¶ *Then shall be sung the*

Sanctus.

THE HOLY COMMUNION.

THE HOLY COMMUNION.

THE HOLY COMMUNION.

¶ *Then may the Minister give* Exhortation *to those that be minded to receive the Lord's Supper, after which, turning to the Altar, and extending his hands over the Bread and Wine, he shall say:*

The Lord's Prayer.

¶ *Then shall the Congregation sing:*

Then shall the Minister say:

"Our Lord Jesus Christ, in the night in which He was betrayed, took bread, etc.;" *ending*—"this do, as oft as ye drink it, in remembrance of Me."

¶ *Then shall be sung the*

Agnus Dei.

A - men.

AGNUS DEI. No. I.

Adagio. con espressione.

O Christ, Thou Lamb of God, Thou Lamb of God, that tak'st a-way the sins of the world, have mer-cy up-on us!

O Christ, Thou Lamb of God, Thou Lamb of God, that tak'st a-way the

THE HOLY COMMUNION.

AGNUS DEI. No. II. Chant No. IV.

O CHRIST, Thou Lamb of God, that takest away..the | sins.. | of..the | world, ||
Have.. | mer-cy | up-on | us!

O Christ, Thou Lamb of God, that takest away..the | sins.. | of..the | world, ||
Have.. | mer-cy | up-on | us!

O Christ, Thou Lamb of God, that takest away..the | sins.. | of..the | world, ||
Grant | us.. | Thy.. | peace. || A-men.

THE HOLY COMMUNION.

¶ *When all have communed, the Minister shall reverently cover what remaineth of the elements.*
¶ *Then, all standing, may be sung the*

Nunc Dimittis.

CHANT No. V.

LORD, now lettest Thou Thy ser-vant de- | part..in | peace : ‖
    Ac- | cord-ing | to..Thy | word :
For mine eyes have seen | Thy..sal- | vation: ‖
    Which Thou hast prepared before..the | face.. | of..all | people ;
A light..to | lighten..the | Gentiles : ‖
    And the glo-ry | of..Thy | peo-ple | Israel.
Glory be to the Fa-ther, | and..to the | Son, ‖ and | to..the | Ho-ly | Ghost:
    As it was in the beginning, is now, and | ever..shall | be, ‖
    World | with-out | end. A- | men.

The Thanksgiving.

Min. O give thanks unto the Lord, for He is good.

Min. Almighty God, our Heavenly Father, we most heartily thank Thee, etc.; *ending:* through Jesus Christ, Thy dear Son our Lord, who liveth and reigneth with Thee, in the unity of the Holy Spirit, world without end.

¶ *The Congregation shall sing:*

THE HOLY COMMUNION.

¶ *Then may be sung a* Doxology, *after which the Minister shall say:*

Blessed be the Name of the Lord.

¶ *The Congregation shall sing or say:*

Minister:

The Lord bless thee, and keep thee.
The Lord make His face shine upon thee, and be gracious unto thee.
The Lord lift up His countenance upon thee, and give thee peace.

¶ *The Congregation shall sing:*

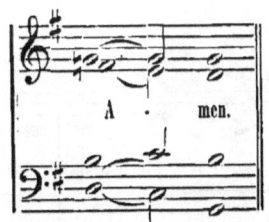

Or this.

THE HOLY COMMUNION.

POST BENEDICTION.

THE HOLY COMMUNION.

ANOTHER FORM.

Minister. The Lord be with you.

Min. Lift up your hearts.

Min. Let us give thanks unto our Lord God.

Therefore with Angels and Archangels, and all the company of Heaven, we laud and magnify thy glorious Name; evermore praising Thee, and saying:

¶ *Then shall be sung the*

Sanctus.

THE HOLY COMMUNION.

SANCTUS. No. I.   ARR. FROM MOSENTHAL.

THE HOLY COMMUNION.

SANCTUS. No. II. *From J. S. Bach, 1736.*

THE HOLY COMMUNION.

AGNUS DEI. No. I.

O CHRIST, Thou Lamb of God, That takest away..the | sins— | of..the | world, ‖
Have.. | mer-cy | up-on | us. ‖

O Christ, Thou Lamb of | God, ‖ That takest away..the | sins— | of..the | world, ‖
Have.. | mer-cy | up-on | us. ‖

O Christ, Thou | Lamb of | God, ‖ That takest away..the | sins— | of..the | world, ‖
Grant | us— | Thy— | peace. ‖ A-men.

AGNUS DEI. No. II.

O CHRIST, Thou Lamb of God, that takest away..the | sins..of the | world, ‖
Have.. | mer-cy | up-on | us.

O Christ, Thou Lamb of God, that takest away..the | sins..of the | world, ‖
Have | mer-cy | up-on | us.

O Christ, Thou Lamb of God, that takest away..the | sins..of the | world, ‖
Grant | us— | Thy— | peace. ‖ A-men.

THE HOLY COMMUNION.

NUNC DIMITTIS,

LORD, now lettest Thou Thy ser-vant de- | part..in | peace: ‖
   Ac- | cord-ing | to..Thy | word:
For mine eyes have seen | Thy..sal- | vation: ‖
Which Thou hast prepared before..the | face— | of..all | people;
A light..to | lighten..the | Gentiles: ‖ And the glo-ry | of..Thy | peo-ple | Israel.
Glory be to the Fa-ther, | and..to the | Son, And | to..the | Ho-ly | Ghost:
As it was in the beginning, is now, and | ever..shall | be, ‖ World | with-out | end.
   A- | men.

The Thanksgiving.

Min. O give thanks unto the Lord, for He is good.

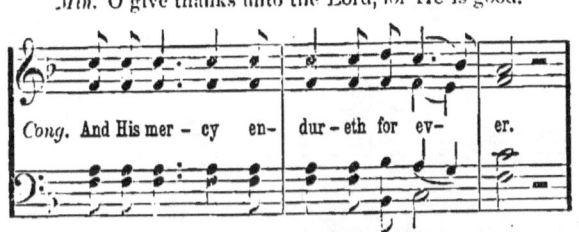 

Min. Blessed be the name of the Lord.

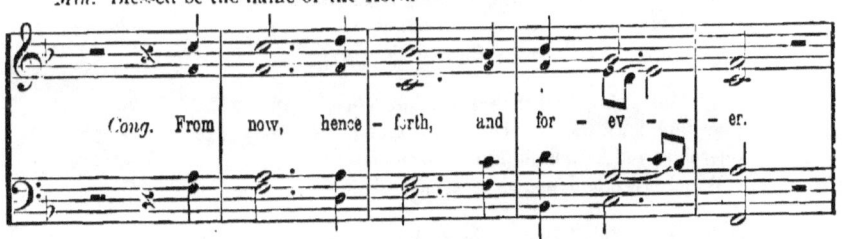

After the Benediction.

 Or,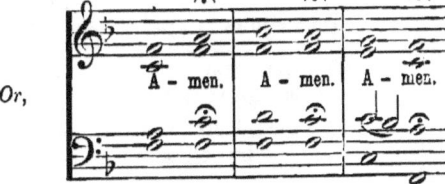

—37—

THE HOLY COMMUNION.

POST BENEDICTION. Rev. J. B. Dykes.

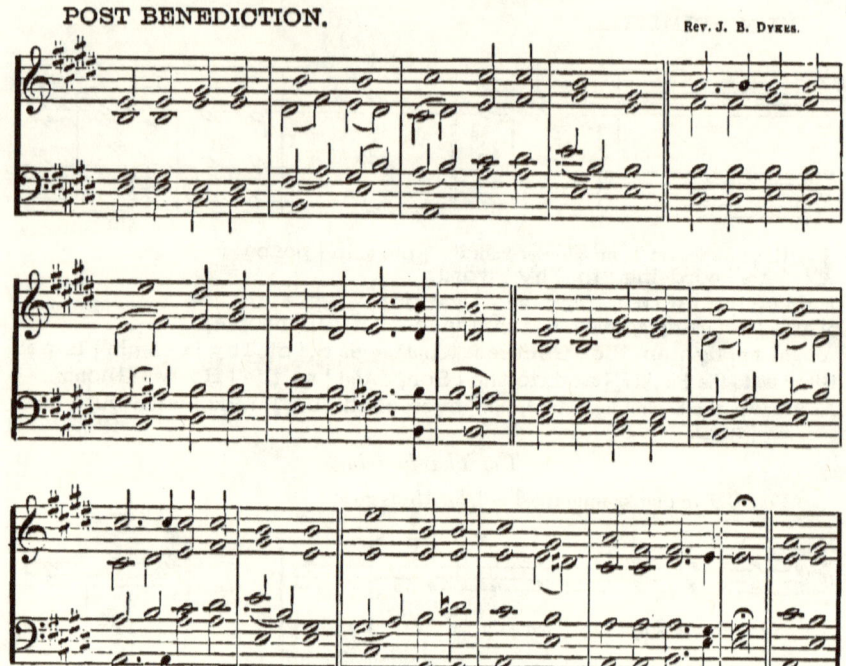

Holy, Holy, Holy! Lord God Almighty!
  Early in the morning our song shall rise to Thee:
Holy, Holy, Holy! merciful and mighty;
  God in Three Persons, Blessèd Trinity

Holy, Holy, Holy! all the saints adore Thee,
  Casting down their golden crowns around the glassy sea:
Cherubim and Seraphim falling down before Thee,
  Which wert, and art, and evermore shalt be.

Holy, Holy, Holy! though the darkness hide Thee,
  Though the eye of sinful man Thy glory may not see.
Only Thou art Holy: there is none beside Thee
  Perfect in power, in love, and purity.

Holy, Holy, Holy! Lord God Almighty!
  All Thy works shall praise Thy Name, in earth, and sky, and sea;
Holy, Holy, Holy! merciful and mighty;
  God in Three Persons, Blessèd Trinity! Amen.

Order of Evening Service.

¶ *The Service shall begin with one of the following* Invitatories. *The Minister, standing before the Altar, may say the Invitatory, and the Congregation sing or say the* Gloria Patri; *or the* Invitatory, *with the* Gloria Patri, *may be said or sung responsively by the Minister and Congregation, or be sung by both together.*

¶ *Any suitable* Psalm *from the* Selections *which precede the* Hymns *may be used as an* Invitatory.

¶ *The* Invitatory, *except in the week before* Easter, *shall always end with the* Gloria Patri.

The Invitatory.

DEUS MISEREATUR.   Chants Nos. VI., VII.

   p GOD be merciful un-to | us,..and | bless us: ‖
      And cause His face..to | shine.. | up-on | us.

   That Thy way may..be | known..upon | earth: ‖
      Thy sav-ing | health..a- | mong..all | nations.

  f Let the people praise | Thee,..O | God: ‖
      Let all..the | peo-ple | praise.. | Thee.

   Then shall the earth | yield..her | increase: ‖
      And God, even our..own | God,..shall | bless.. | us.

 pp God..shall | bless.. | us: ‖
      And all the ends..of the | earth..shall | fear.. | Him.

   Glory be to the Fa-ther, | and..to the | Son, ‖
      And | to..the | Ho-ly | Ghost:

   As it was in the beginning,..is now,..and | ever..shall | be, ‖
      World | with-out | end.   A- | men.

EVENING SERVICE.

JUBILATE DEO. Chant No. VIII.

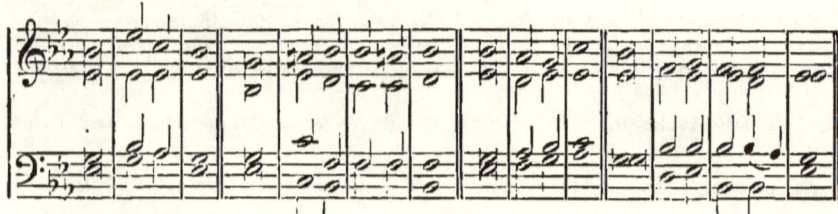

JUBILATE DEO. Chants Nos. IX., X.

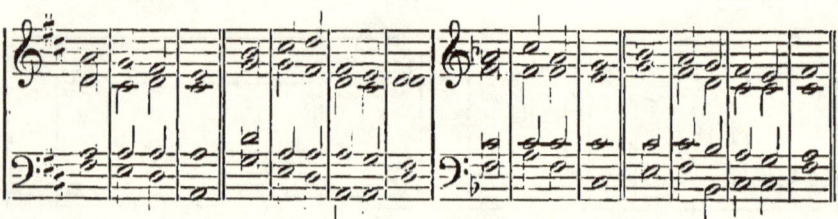

f MAKE a joyful noise unto the Lord,..all | **ye..**— | **lands:** ||
    Serve the Lord with gladness, come before.. His | **presence..with** | **sing-** | **ing.**
Know ye that the Lord | **He..is** | **God ;** ||
    It is He that hath made us, and not we ourselves...we are His people,..and the | **sheep..** | **of..His** | **pasture.**
Enter into His gates with thanksgiving, and in-..to His | **courts..with** | **praise:** ||
    Be thankful unto Him,..and | **bless..** | **His..** | **Name.**
For..the | **Lord..is** | **good ;** || .
    His mercy is everlasting; and His truth endur-eth to | **all..** | **gen-er-** | **ations.**
Glory be to the Fa-ther, | **and.. to the..** | **Son,** ||
    And | **to..the** | **Ho-ly** | **Ghost:**
As it was in the beginning, is now, and | **ever..shall** | **be,** ||
    World | **with-out** | **end.   A-** | **men.**

VENITE EXULTEMUS DOMINO. Chants Nos. XI., XII.

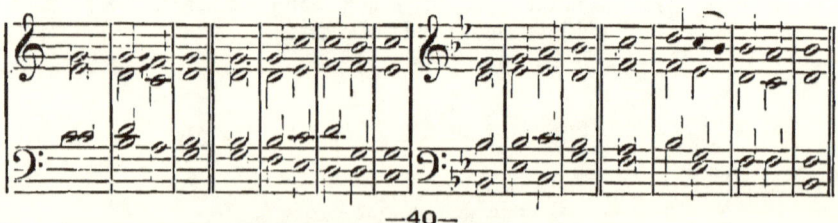

EVENING SERVICE.

f O COME, let us sing..un- | to..the | Lord : ‖
　　Let us make a joyful noise..to the | Rock..of | our..sal- | vation.
　Let us come before His pre-sence | with..thanks- | giving : ‖
　　And make a joyful noise..unto | Him.. | with.. | psalms.
　For the Lord..is a | great.. | God : ‖
　　And a great | King..a- | bove..all | gods.
mf In His hand are the deep pla-ces | of..the | earth : ‖
　　The strength of the hills..is | His.. | al..- | so.
　The sea is His, | and..He | made it : ‖
　　And His hands | formed..the | dry.. | land.
　O come, let us wor-ship | and..bow | down : ‖
　　Let us kneel..be- | fore..the | Lord..our | Maker.
　For..He | is..our | God : ‖
　　And we are the people of His pas-ture, and the | sheep.. | of..His | hand.
　Glory be to the Fa-ther, | and..to the | Son, ‖
　　And | to..the | Ho-ly | Ghost :
　As it was in the beginning, is now, and | ever..shall | be, ‖
　　World | with-out | end.　A- | men.

LAETATUS SUM.　Chants Nos. XIII., XIV.

mf I WAS glad when they said unto me, Let us go into the house | of..the | Lord : ‖
　　Our feet shall stand within thy gates, | O..Je- | ru-sa- | lem.
p Pray for the peace..of Je- | ru-sa- | lem : ‖
　　They.. shall | prosper..that | love.. | thee.
pp Peace..be with- | in..thy | walls : ‖
　　And prosperity.. | with-.. | in..thy | palaces.
　Glory be to the Fa-ther, | and..to the | Son, ‖
　　And | to..the | Ho-ly | Ghost :
　As it was in the beginning, is now, and | ever..shall | be, ‖
　　World | with-out | end.　A- | men.

EVENING SERVICE.

LAVABO INTER INNOCENTES. Chants Nos. XV., XVI.

mf I WILL wash mine hands..in | **inno-cen-** | **cy:** ‖
So will I compass..Thine | **Al-tar,** | **O..** | **Lord.**

That I may publish with the voice | **of..thanks-** | **giving:** ‖
And tell..of | **all..Thy** | **wond-rous** | **works.**

Lord, I have loved the habita..tion | **of..Thy** | **house:**
And the place where Thine | **hon-or** | **dwell—** | **eth.**

Glory be to the Fa-ther, | **and..to the** | **Son,** ‖
And | **to..the** | **Ho-ly** | **Ghost:** ‖

As it was in the beginning, is now, and | **ever..shall** | **be,** ‖
World.. | **with-out** | **end. A-** | **men.**

The Confession of Sins.

DEARLY BELOVED! If we say that we have no sin, we deceive ourselves, and the truth is not in us. But if we confess our sins, God is faithful and just to forgive us our sins and to cleanse us from all unrighteousness. Let us therefore confess our sins unto God our heavenly Father, and humbly beseech Him, in the Name of our Lord Jesus Christ, to grant us forgiveness.

ALMIGHTY and most merciful Father; we poor miserable sinners acknowledge and confess our manifold sins and wickedness, which we, from time to time, most grievously have committed, by thought, word, and deed, against Thy Divine Majesty. We have provoked Thy wrath and indignation against us, and deserve at Thy hands present and everlasting punishment. But we do earnestly repent, and are heartily sorry for these our misdoings; and we beseech Thee, of Thy great goodness, to be merciful unto us. *Pardon and deliver us from all our sins, for the sake of the holy, innocent, and bitter sufferings and death of Thy dear Son, Jesus Christ our Lord.*

☞ *Then shall the Congregation sing the*
Kyrie.

pp Lord, have mer-cy upon us! *p* Christ, have mer-cy upon us! *mf* Lord, have mer-cy up - on us!

Or this:

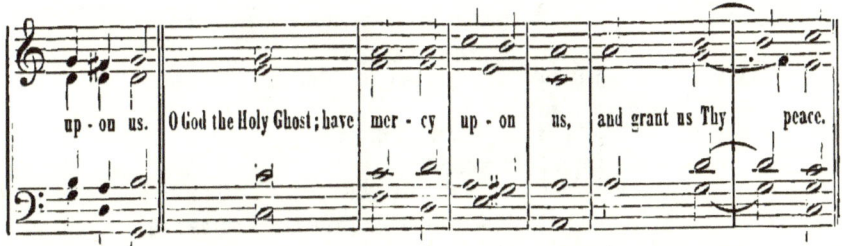

℟ *Then the Minister, standing, shall pronounce*

The Absolution,

Ending, *He that believeth, and is baptized, shall be saved. Grant us, O Lord, this salvation.*

¶ *Then shall the Congregation sing:*

Min. O Lord, open Thou my lips.

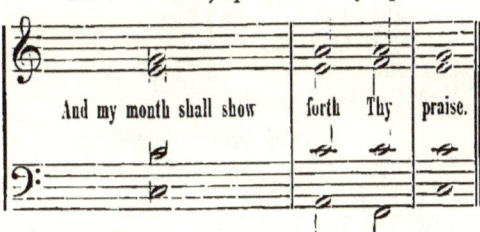

℟ *Then shall be sung the* Magnificat, *as here followeth;* or some other Canticle, Psalm, or Hymn of Praise; and at the end of the Canticle or Psalm may be sung the Gloria Patri. *The Minister shall say the first words.*

EVENING SERVICE.

Min. My soul doth magnify the Lord.

THE MAGNIFICAT. Chants Nos. XVII., XVIII.

f MY soul doth mag-ni- | fy..the | Lord: ||
And my spirit hath..re- | joiced..in | God my | Saviour.

For..He | hath..re- | garded : ||
The low estate..of | His.. | hand-.. | maiden.

For..be- | hold,.. from | henceforth: ||
All..gener- | ations..shall | call..me | blessed.

For He that is mighty hath done..to me | great..— | things : ||
And | ho-ly | is..His | Name.

mf And His mer-cy is on | them..that | fear Him : ||
From ge-ner- | ation..to | gen-er- | ation.

He hath showed strength | with..His | arm : ||
ff He hath scattered the proud in the ima-gin- | a..tion | of..their | hearts.

mf He hath put down the migh-ty | from..their | seats : ||
And exalt-ed | them..of | low..de- | gree.

He hath filled the hung-ry | with..good | things: ||
And the rich..He hath | sent.. | empty..a- | way.

He hath holpen His servant Israel, in remem-brance | of..His | mercy: ||
As He spake to our fathers, to Abraham,..and | to..His | seed,..for- | ever.

Glory be to the Fa-ther, | and..to the | Son, ||
And | to..the | Ho-ly | Ghost :

As it was in the beginning, is now, and | ever..shall | be, ||
World | with-out | end. A- | men.

¶ *Then shall the Minister say:*

Min. The Lord be with you.

EVENING SERVICE.

¶ *Then shall the Minister say one or more of the festival, general, or special* Collects. *A Versicle may precede the Collect.*

The Collect.

¶ *The Collect ended, the Congregation shall sing:*

A - men.

¶ *Then shall one or more Lessons from the Holy Scriptures be read. If more than one Lesson be read, one of the Sentences after the Epistle in the Morning Service, or a Psalm, may be sung after the first Lesson.*

¶ *The Lessons ended, the Minister shall say:* Here endeth the Scripture (or the second) Lesson, *and the Congregation shall sing:*

DEO GRATIAS. No. I.   Or, DEO GRATIAS. No. II.

Thanks be to Thee, O God.   Thanks be to Thee, O God.

¶ *Then may the Apostles' Creed be said or sung by the Minister and Congregation. When the Creed is used, the Congregation shall stand up at the end of the Scripture Lesson.*

The Apostles' Creed.

I believe in God, etc., | I believe in the Holy | Ghost; The Holy Christian | Church; the Communion of

Saints; The Forgiveness of | sins; The Resurrection of the | body; | And the Life ev-er-last-ing. | A-men.

EVENING SERVICE.

¶ *Then shall the Minister announce the Hymn to be sung, and go into the pulpit. After the Hymn shall follow*

The Sermon.

¶ *When the Sermon is ended, the Congregation all standing up, and continuing to stand to the end of the Lord's Prayer, the Minister shall say:*

The grace of the Lord Jesus Christ, and the love of God, and the communion of the Holy Ghost, be with you all.

¶ *Then shall the Congregation sing:*

ƒ I WILL praise the Lord..with | my..whole | heart: ‖
In the assembly of the upright,...and | in..the | con-gre- | gation.

He hath made His wonderful works..to | be..re- | membered : ‖
The Lord is gra-cious and | full.. | of..com- | passion.

He sent redemp..tion un- | to..His | people : ‖
Ho-ly and | rev-erend | is..His | Name.

¶ *Whilst this is sung, the Minister shall go to the Altar, and the singing ended, he shall offer prayer; he may use the Litany, or the Suffrages, or a selection from the Collects, or any suitable prayer.*

The Prayer.

¶ *Then shall the Minister, and the Congregation with him, say the Lord's Prayer.*

¶ *Then may the Minister make any needful announcements, and the Offerings of the Congregation be gathered; and after that shall follow a Hymn which shall end with a Doxology. Whilst the Doxology is sung the Congregation shall stand.*

¶ *When the Doxology is ended, the Minister, standing before the Altar, shall pronounce the Benediction, after which the Congregation, still standing, should offer silent prayer.*

The Benediction.

The Lord bless thee, and keep thee.
The Lord make His face shine upon thee, and be gracious unto thee.
The Lord lift up His countenance upon thee, and give thee peace.

¶ *The Congregation shall sing:*

The Litany.

¶ *The Litany may be used at Evening Service on Sundays, Wednesdays, and Fridays, on Days of Humiliation and Prayer, and at Morning Service on Sundays when there is no Communion. The responses may be repeated after each phrase, or only at the end of each group, as here followeth:*

    Min. Lord, have mercy upon us.   *Min.* Christ, have mercy upon us.

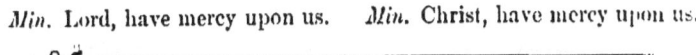

    Min. Lord, have mercy upon us.   *Min.* O Christ, hear us.

O God, the Father in heaven;..............

O God the Son, Redeemer of the world;..

O God, the Holy Ghost;.....................

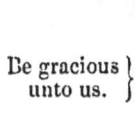 Be gracious unto us.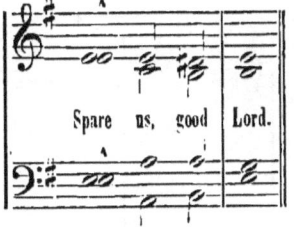

Be gracious unto us.

—47—

THE LITANY.

From all sin;
From all error;
From all evil:

Good Lord, deliver us.

From the crafts and assaults of the devil;
From sudden and evil death;
From pestilence and famine;
From war and bloodshed;
From sedition and rebellion;
From lightning and tempest;
From all calamity by fire and water;
And from everlasting death:

Good Lord, deliver us.

By the mystery of Thy holy Incarnation;
By Thy holy Nativity;
By Thy Baptism, Fasting, and Temptation;
By Thine Agony and Bloody Sweat;
By Thy Cross and Passion;
By Thy precious Death and Burial;
By Thy glorious Resurrection and Ascension;
And by the coming of the Holy Ghost, the Comforter:

Help us, good Lord.

In all time of our tribulation;
In all time of our prosperity;
In the hour of death;
And in the day of judgment:

We poor sinners do beseech Thee:

To hear us, O Lord God.

THE LITANY.

And to rule and govern Thy holy Christian Church;
To preserve all pastors and ministers of Thy Church in the true knowledge and understanding of Thy Word, and in holiness of life;
To put an end to all schisms and causes of offence;
To bring into the way of truth all such as have erred, and are deceived;
To beat down Satan under our feet;
To send faithful laborers into Thy harvest;
To accompany Thy Word with Thy Spirit and grace;
To raise up them that fall, and to strengthen such as do stand;
And to comfort and help the weak-hearted and the distressed:

To give to all nations peace and concord;
To preserve our country from discord and contention;
To give to our nation perpetual victory over all its enemies;
To direct and defend our President, and all in authority;
And to bless and keep our magistrates, and all our people:

To behold and succor all who are in danger, necessity, and tribulation;
To protect all who travel by land or water;
To preserve all women in the perils of childbirth;
To strengthen and keep all sick persons and young children;
To set free all who are innocently imprisoned;
To defend and provide for all fatherless children and widows;
And to have mercy upon all men:

To forgive our enemies, persecutors, and slanderers, and to turn their hearts;
To give and preserve to our use the fruits of the earth;
And graciously to hear our prayers:

THE LITANY.

O Lord Jesus Christ, Son of God;

O Lamb of God, that takest away the sins of the world;
O Lamb of God, that takest away the sins of the world;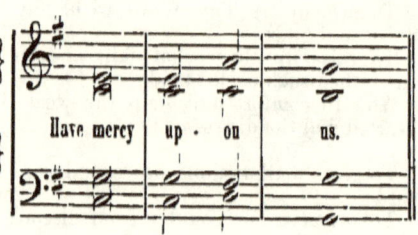

O Lamb of God, that takest away the sins of the world,  O Christ, hear us.

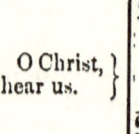

Lord, have mercy upon us..............
Christ, have mercy upon us..............
Lord, have mercy upon us..............

THE LITANY.

¶ *Then shall the Minister, and the Congregation with him, say the Lord's Prayer, after which may be said one or more of the Litany Collects here following.*

¶ *After each Collect the Amen may be sung, using the same form each time.*

A - men.

Litany Collects.

Minister.

O Lord, deal not with us after our sins.

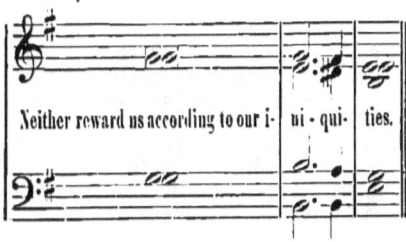
Neither reward us according to our i- ni - qui - ties.

ALMIGHTY GOD, our heavenly Father, Who desirest not the death of a sinner, but rather that he should turn from his evil way and live; We beseech Thee graciously to turn from us those punishments which we by our sins have deserved, and to grant us grace ever hereafter to serve Thee in holiness and pureness of living; through Jesus Christ our Lord. Amen.

Min. Help us, O God of our salvation, for the glory of Thy Name.

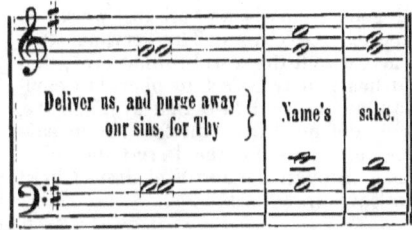
Deliver us, and purge away our sins, for Thy Name's sake.

ALMIGHTY and everlasting God, Who by Thy Holy Spirit dost govern and sanctify the whole Christian Church; Hear our prayers for all members of the same, and mercifully grant, that by Thy grace they may serve Thee in true faith; through Jesus Christ Thy Son our Lord. Amen.

Min. O Lord, deal not with us after our sins.

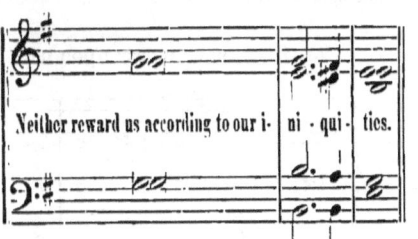
Neither reward us according to our i- ni - qui - ties.

O GOD, merciful Father, Who despisest not the sighing of a contrite heart, nor the desire of such as are sorrowful; Mercifully assist our prayers which we make before Thee in all our troubles and adversities, whensoever they oppress us; and graciously hear us, that those evils which the craft and subtilty of the devil or man worketh against us, may, by Thy good providence, be brought to nought; that we Thy servants, being hurt by no persecutions, may evermore give thanks unto Thee in Thy holy Church; through Jesus Christ Thy Son our Lord. Amen.

THE LITANY.

Min. O Lord, enter not into judgment with Thy servant.

ALMIGHTY GOD, Who knowest us to be set in the midst of so many and great dangers, that by reason of the frailty of our nature we cannot always stand upright; Grant to us such strength and protection, as may support us in all dangers, and carry us through all temptations; through Jesus Christ our Lord. *Amen.*

Min. Call upon me in the day of trouble.

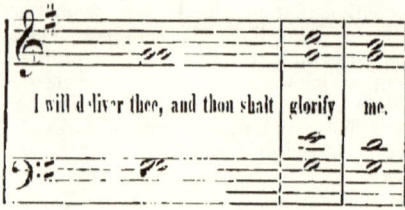

SPARE us, O Lord, and mercifully forgive us our sins, and though by our continual transgressions we have merited Thy punishments, be gracious unto us, and grant that all those evils which we have deserved, may be turned from us, and overruled to our everlasting good; through Jesus Christ Thy Son our Lord. *Amen.*

Min. The Lord will give strength unto His people.

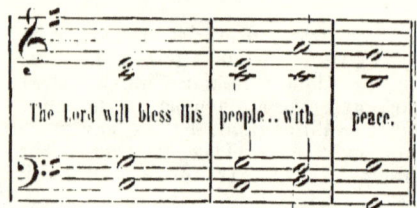

O GOD, from Whom all holy desires, all good counsels, and all just works do proceed; Give unto Thy servants that peace, which the world cannot give; that our hearts may be set to obey Thy commandments, and also that by Thee, we, being defended from the fear of our enemies, may pass our time in rest and quietness; through the merits of Jesus Christ our Saviour. *Amen.*

The Suffrages.

The Suffrages may be used in the same manner as the Litany.

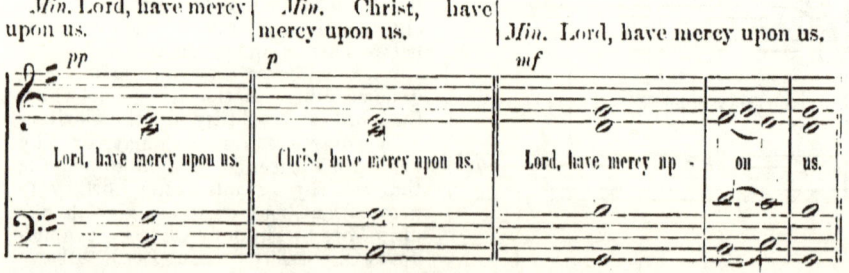

THE SUFFRAGES.

Our Father, who art in heaven; hallowed be Thy Name; Thy kingdom come; Thy will be done on earth, as it is in heaven; give us this day our daily bread; and forgive us our trespasses, as we forgive those who trespass against us; and lead us not into temptation;

But deliver us from evil.

Min. I said: O Lord, be merciful unto me. | *Min.* Return, O Lord, how long?

Heal my soul, for I have sinned against Thee. And let it repent Thee concerning Thy servants.

Min. Let Thy mercy, O Lord, be upon us. | *Min.* Let Thy priests be clothed with righteousness.

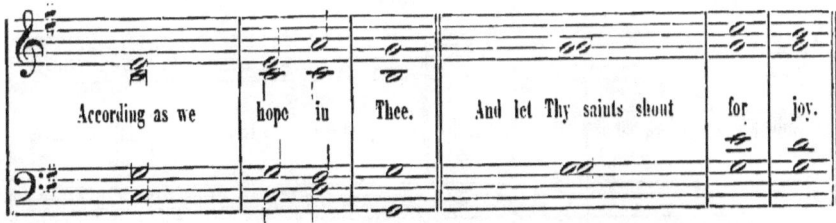

According as we hope in Thee. And let Thy saints shout for joy.

Min. O Lord, our King, save us. | *Min.* Save Thy people, and bless Thine inheritance.

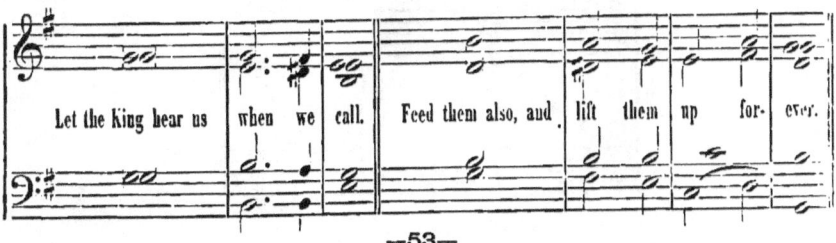

Let the King hear us when we call. Feed them also, and lift them up forever.

THE SUFFRAGES.

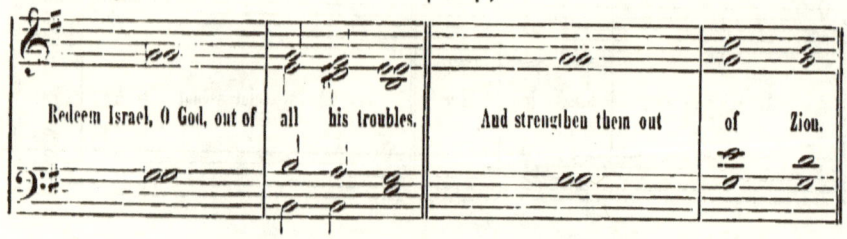

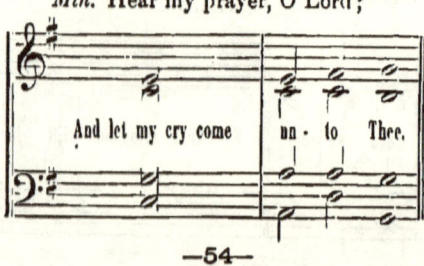

THE SUFFRAGES.

At Morning Service.

DE PROFUNDIS. Chant No. XXI.

pp **O**UT of the depths have..I.. | **cried:** ‖
  Unto Thee, O.. | **Lord.**‖

  Lord, hear..my.. | **voice:** ‖
  Let Thine ears be attentive to the voice..of my..suppli- | **cations.** ‖

  If Thou, Lord, shouldst mark..iniqui- | **ties:** ‖
  O Lord,..who shall | **stand?** ‖

  But there is forgiveness..with | **Thee:** ‖
  That Thou mayest..be | **feared.** ‖

  I wait for the Lord, my soul..doth | **wait:** ‖
  And in His word..do I | **hope.** ‖

  My soul waiteth for the Lord more than they that watch..for the | **morning:** ‖
  I say, more than they that watch..for the | **morning.** ‖

  Let Israel hope in the Lord, for with the Lord..there is | **mercy:** ‖
  And with Him is plenteous..re- | **demption.** ‖

  And He shall redeem..Is- | **rael:** ‖
  From all his iniqui- | **ties.** ‖

THE SUFFRAGES.

At Evening Service.

MISERERE MEI. Chant No. XXII.

p **H**AVE mercy upon me, O God, accord-ing to Thy | lov-ing | kindness : ‖
According unto the multitude of Thy tender mer-cies blot | out.. | my.. trans- | gressions.

Wash me thoroughly..from | mine..in- | iquity : ‖
And | cleanse..me | from..my | sin.

For I acknow-ledge | my..trans- | gressions : ‖
And my sin..is | ever..be- | fore.. | me.

Against Thee, Thee only, have I sinned and done this e-vil | in..Thy | sight : ‖
That Thou mightest be justified when Thou speakest, and be clear | when.. | Thou.. | judgest.

Purge me with hyssop and..I | shall..be | clean : ‖
Wash me, and I shall..be | whi-ter | than.. | snow.

Make me to hear | joy..and | gladness : ‖
That the bones which Thou hast | bro-ken | may re- | joice.

Hide Thy face | from..my | sins : ‖
And blot out all..of | mine..in- | i-qui- | ties.

Create in me..a clean | heart,..O | God : ‖
And renew..a right | spirit..with- | in.. | me.

Cast me not away | from..Thy | presence : ‖
And take not Thy | Ho-ly | Spir-it | from me.

Restore unto me the joy..of | Thy..sal- | vation : ‖
And uphold..me | with.. | Thy free | Spirit.

f Then will I teach..trans- | gressors..Thy | ways ; ‖
And sinners shall be..con- | vert-ed | un-to | Thee.

ff O Lord, o-pen | Thou..my | lips : ‖
And my mouth..shall show | forth.. | Thy.. | praise.

mf For Thou desi-rest not | sa-cri- | fice ; ‖
Else would I give it : Thou delight-est | not..in | burnt.. | offering.

The sacrifices of God..are a | bro-ken | spirit : ‖
A broken and a contrite heart, O God, Thou | wilt.. | not..des- | pise.

THE SUFFRAGES.

Min. Turn us again, O God of hosts.

Min. Arise, O Christ, for our help;

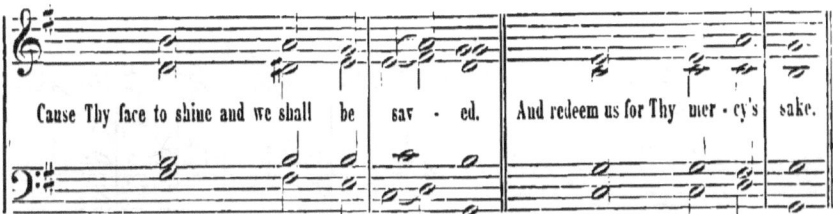

Min. Hear my prayer, O Lord;

Min. The Lord be with you.

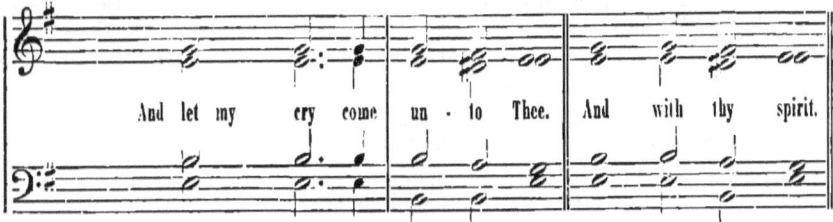

Let us pray.

¶ *Then may the Minister say a* Collect *for the Season and any other suitable* Collects, *and after that he may say this* Collect *for peace.*

Min. Give peace in our days, O Lord:

Min. O Lord, let there be peace in Thy strength;

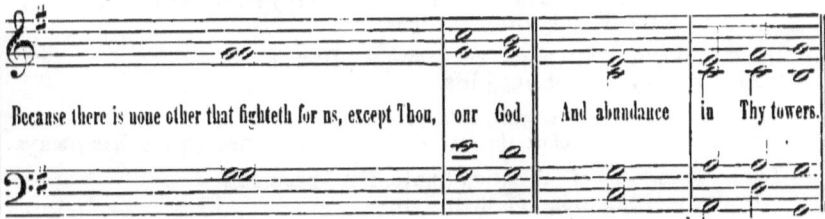

Let us pray.

O GOD, from Whom all holy desires, all good counsels, and all just works do proceed; Give unto Thy servants that peace which the world cannot give, that our hearts may be set to obey Thy commandments, *and also that by Thee, we being defended from the fear of our enemies, may pass our time in rest and quietness;* through the merits of Jesus Christ our Saviour.

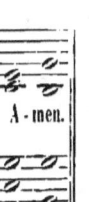

Min. Blessed be the Name of the Lord.

Canticles.

BENEDICTUS. Chant No. XXIII.

mf **B**LESSED be the Lord | God..of | Israel: ‖
For He hath visited | and..re- | deemed His | people.

And hath raised up a horn of sal- | va-tion | for us: ‖
In the house..of His | ser-vant | Da- — | vid:

As He spake by the mouth..of His | ho-ly | prophets: ‖
Which have been | since..the | world..be- | gan:

That we should be sav-ed | from..our | enemies: ‖
And from..the | hand..of | all..that | hate us:

To perform the mercy promised | to..our | fathers: ‖
And to..re- | member..His | ho-ly | covenant:

The oath which He sware to our fa-ther | A-bra- | ham: ‖
That He would | grant — | un-to | us:

That we, being delivered out of the hand | of..our | enemies: ‖
Might | serve..Him | with-out | fear,

In holiness and righteousness be- | fore — | Him: ‖
All..the | days — | of..our | life.

f And thou, child, shalt be called the pro-phet | of..the | Highest: ‖
For thou shalt go before the face..of the | Lord..to pre- | pare..His | ways:

To give knowledge of salva..tion | unto..His | people: ‖
By..the re- | mis-sion | of..their | sins,

Through the tender mer-cy | of..our | God: ‖
Whereby the day-spring from on | high..hath | visit-ed | us,

To give light to them that sit in darkness and in..the | shadow..of | death: ‖
To guide our feet | into..the | way..of | peace.

ff Glory be to the Fa-ther, | and..to the | Son, ‖
And | to..the | Ho-ly | Ghost:

As it was in the beginning, is now, and | ever..shall | be, ‖
World | with-out | end. A- | men.

—58—

CANTICLES.

BENEDICTUS. Chant No. XXIV.

BENEDICITE. Chant No. XXV.

mf O ALL ye works of the Lord, bless | ye..the | Lord : ‖
Praise..Him, and | magni-fy | Him..for- | ever.

ff O ye Angels of the Lord, bless | ye..the | Lord : ‖
Praise..Him, and | **magni-fy** | **Him..for-** | **ever.**

O ye Heavens, bless | **ye..the** | **Lord :** ‖
Praise..Him, and | **magni-fy** | **Him..for-** | **ever.**

O all ye Powers of the Lord, bless | ye..the | Lord : ‖
Praise..Him, and | **magni-fy** | **Him..for-** | **ever.**

O let the Earth | **bless..the** | **Lord :** ‖
Yea, let it praise..Him, and | **magni-fy** | **Him..for-** | **ever.**

O ye Children of Men, bless | ye..the | Lord : ‖
Praise..Him, and | **magni-fy** | **Him..for-** | **ever.**

O let Israel | **bless..the** | **Lord :** ‖
Praise..Him, and | **magni-fy** | **Him..for-** | **ever.**

O ye Priests of the Lord, bless | ye..the | Lord : ‖
Praise..Him, and | **magni-fy** | **Him..for-** | **ever.**

O ye Servants of the Lord, bless | ye..the | Lord : ‖
Praise..Him, and | **magni-fy** | **Him..for-** | **ever.**

O ye Spirits and Souls of the righteous, bless | ye..the | Lord : ‖
Praise..Him, and | **magni-fy** | **Him..for-** | **ever.**

O ye Holy and Humble Men of heart, bless | ye..the | Lord : ‖
Praise..Him, and | **magni-fy** | **Him..for-** | **ever.**

We bless the Father and the Son and the | **Ho-ly** | **Ghost :** ‖
We praise Him,..and | **magni-fy** | **Him..for-** | **ever.**

CANTICLES.

TE DEUM LAUDAMUS. Chant No. XXVI.

A.—f WE praise Thee, O God: we acknowledge Thee to | **be the** | **Lord.** ||
All the earth doth worship Thee, the | **Fath-er** | **ever-** | **lasting.**

ff To Thee all angels | **cry a-** | **loud;** ||
The heavens, and | **all the** | **powers..there-** | **in.**

A.— To Thee, Cherubim and | **Sera-** | **phim** || con- | **tinual-** | ly do | cry,
pp Holy, Holy, Holy, Lord | **God of** | **Sabaoth;** ||
ff Heaven and earth are full of the | **ma-jesty** | **of Thy** | **glory.**

B.— The glorious company of the Apostles | **praise —** | **Thee.**
The goodly fellowship of the Prophets | **praise —** | **Thee.**
The noble army of Martyrs | **praise —** | **Thee.**
mf The holy Church throughout all the world doth ac- | **knowledge** | **Thee;** ||
The Father, of an | **in-finite** | **Majes-** | **ty.**

CANTICLES.

C.—Thine adorable, true, and | **only** | **Son;** ‖
  Also the Holy | **Ghost, the** | **Comfort-** | **er.**

A.—*ff* Thou art the King of Glory, | **O —** | **Christ.** ‖
  Thou art the everlasting | **Son —** | **of the** | **Father.**

  p When Thou tookest upon Thee to de- | **liver** | **man,** ‖
  Thou didst humble Thyself to be | **born of a** | **vir- —** | **gin.**

A.—When Thou hadst overcome the | **sharpness..of** | **death,** ‖
  Thou didst open the kingdom of | **heaven..to** | **all be-** | **lievers.**

  f Thou sittest at the right | **hand of** | **God** ‖
  In the | **glory** | **of the** | **Father.**

B.—We believe that Thou shalt come to | **be our** | **Judge.** ‖ [*omit repeat.*]
  We therefore pray Thee, help Thy servants, whom Thou hast redeemed |
  with Thy | **precious** | **blood.**

C.—Make them to be numbered | **with Thy** | **saints** ‖ in | **glory** | **ever-** | **lasting.**

A.—O Lord, save Thy people, and | **bless Thine** | **heritage.** ‖
  Govern them, and | **lift them** | **up for-** | **ever.**

  ff Day by day we | **mag-nify** | **Thee.** ‖
  And we worship Thy Name | **ever,** | **world without** | **end.**

A.—Vouchsafe, O Lord, to keep us this day | **without** | **sin.** ‖
  O Lord, have mercy upon us; have | **mercy** | **upon** | **us.**

  O Lord, let Thy mercy be upon us, as our | **trust..is in** | **Thee.** ‖
  ff O Lord, in Thee have I trusted, let me | **never** | **be con-** | **founded.** Amen.

DIGNUS EST AGNUS. Chant No. XXVII.

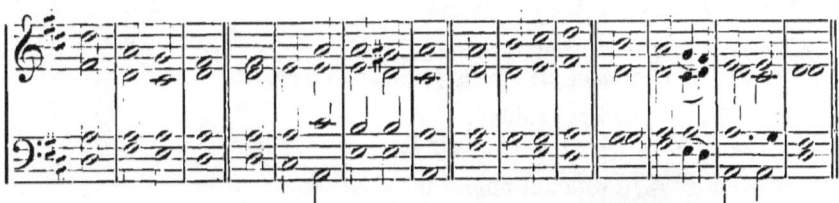

f WORTHY is the Lamb that was slain to receive power, and ri-ches, | **and..**
  And strength, and | **honor..and** | **glory..and** | **blessing.** [**wis-** | **dom :** ‖
  Blessing and honor, and | **glory..and** | **power,** ‖
  Be unto Him that sitteth upon the throne: and un-to the | **Lamb..for-** | **ever..**
  and | **ever.**
  Great and marvellous are Thy works, Lord | **God..Al-** | **mighty :** ‖
  Just and true are Thy | **ways..Thou** | **King..of** | **Saints.**
  Who shall not fear Thee, O Lord, and glo-ri- | **fy..Thy** | **name ?** ‖
  For Thou | **only..art** | **ho- —** | **ly.**
  ff Praise ye our God, all | **ye..His** | **servants,** ‖
  And ye that fear..Him both | **small —** | **and —** | **great.**
  fff Alleluia ! for the Lord God..Om- | **nipo-tent** ; **reigneth.** ‖
  Alleluia ! | **Al-le-** | **lu- —** | **ia !** ‖ : Amen.

Psalms.

BENEDIC ANIMA. Chant No. XXVIII.

f **B**LESS the Lord, | O..my | soul: ‖
   And all that is within me | bless..His | ho-ly | Name.

  Bless the Lord, O..my | soul: ‖
   And forget not | all..His | ben-e- | fits:

mf Who forgiv-eth all | thine..in- | iquities: ‖
   Who heal-eth | all — | thy..dis- | eases:

  Who redeemeth thy life | from..des- | truction:
   Who crowneth thee with loving-kindness and | ten-der | mer- — | cies.

  Who satisfieth thy mouth | with..good | things: |
   So that thy youth is..re- | new-ed like..the eagle's.

  The Lord executeth righteousness and | judg- — | ment: ‖
   For | all..that | are..op- pressed.

p The Lord is mer-ciful and | gra- — | cious: |
   Slow to anger, and | plen-teous in | mer- — | cy.

  He will..not al-ways | chide: ‖
   Neither will He keep..His | anger..for- | ev- — | er.

  He hath not dealt with us | after..our | sins: ‖
   Nor rewarded us accord-ing to | our..in- | i-qui- | ties.

f For as the heaven is high..a- bove..the | earth:
   So great is His mercy toward | them..that | fear — | Him.

  As far as the east..is from..the | west: ‖
   So far hath He removed our trans- | gres-sions | from — | us.

PSALMS.

BENEDIC ANIMA. Second Part. Chant No. XXIX.

pp LIKE as a fa-ther | pitieth..his | children : ‖
So the Lord pitieth | them..that | fear — | **Him.**

p For..He | knoweth..our | frame : ‖
He remem-bereth | that — | we..are | dust.

As for man, his days | are..as | grass : ‖
As a flower of the field, | so..he | flou-rish- | eth.

For the wind passeth over it, and | it..is | gone : ‖
And the place thereof..shall | know..it | no — | more.

But the mercy of the Lord is from everlasting to everlast-ing upon | **them..that | fear Him :** ‖
And His right-eousness | un-to | chil-dren's | children ;

To such..as | keep..His | covenant : ‖
And to those that remem-ber His com- | mand-ments to | do — | them.

BENEDIC ANIMA. Third Part. Chant No. XXX.

f THE Lord hath prepared His throne | in..the | heavens : ‖
And His king-dom | ru-leth | o-ver | all.

Bless the Lord, ye His angels, that.. ex- | cel..in | strength : ‖
That do His commandments, hearkening un-to the | voice — | of..His | word.

Bless ye the Lord, all | ye..**His** | hosts : ‖
Ye ministers of His, that | do..**His** | plea- — | sure.

ff Bless the Lord, all His works, in all pla-ces of | **His..do-** | **minion :** ‖
Bless the Lord, | O — | my — | soul.

—63—

PSALMS.

DEUS, JUDICIUM TUUM.   Chant No. XXXI.

mf **G**IVE the king..Thy | judgments..O | God: ||
    And Thy right-eousness un- | to..the | king's — | son.
He shall judge Thy peo-ple with | righ-teous- | ness: ||
    And..Thy | poor..with | judg- — | ment.
The mountains shall bring peace | to..the | people: ||
    And the little | hills..by | righ-teous- | ness.
He shall judge the poor | of..the | people: || [op- | pressor.
    He shall save the children of the needy, and shall break..in | pie-ces | the..
They shall fear Thee as long as the sun..and | moon..en- | dure: ||
    Through-out | all — | ge-ne- | rations.

DEUS, JUDICIUM TUUM.   Second Part.   Chant No. XXXII.

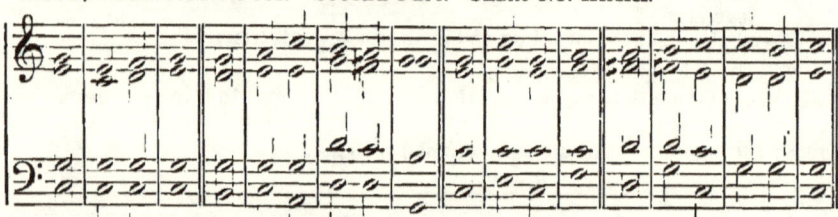

f **H**E shall come down like rain..upon the | mown — | grass: ||
    As showers that | wa- — | ter..the | earth.
In his days..shall the | righ-teous | flourish: ||
    And abundance of peace so long..as the | moon..en- | dur- — | eth.
ff He shall have dominion al-so from | sea..to | sea: ||
    And from the river unto the | ends — | of..the | earth.
They that dwell in the wilderness shall bow..be- | fore — | him: ||
    And his enemies | shall — | lick..the | dust.
The kings of Tarshish and of the isles..shall | bring — | presents: ||
    The kings of Sheba and Seba | shall — | of-fer | gifts.
Yea, all kings shall fall down..be- | fore — | him: ||
    All nations | shall — | serve — | him.
p For he shall deliver the need-y | when..he | crieth: ||
    The poor also, and | him..that | hath..no | helper.
He shall spare..the | poor..and | needy: ||
    And shall save..the | souls — | of..the | needy.
He shall redeem their soul from deceit..and | vi-o- | lence: ||
    And precious shall their | blood..be | in..his | sight.
ff And he shall live, and to him shall be given of the gold..of | She- — | ba: || [ed
    Prayer also shall be made for him continually; and dail-y shall he..be prais- —

PSALMS.

DEUS, JUDICIUM TUUM. Third Part. Chant No. XXXIII.

ff THERE shall be a handful of corn in the earth upon the top of the moun-
tains: the fruit thereof..shall | **shake..like** | **Lebanon** ; ||
And they of the city shall flou-rish like | **grass** — | **of..the** | **earth.**
His name..shall en- | **dure..for-** | **ever** : ||
His name shall be contin-ued as | **long** — | **as..the** | **sun** ;
And men..shall be | **blessed..in** | **Him** : ||
All na-tions shall | **call..Him** | **bless-** — | **ed.**
Blessed be the Lord God, the | **God..of** | **Israel** : ||
Who on-ly | **do-eth** | **won-drous** | **things.**
And blessed be His glo-rious | **name..for-** | **ever** : ||
And let the whole earth be filled with His glory. | **A-men..** | **and..A-** | **men.**

DEUS MISEREATUR. Chant No. **XXXIV.**

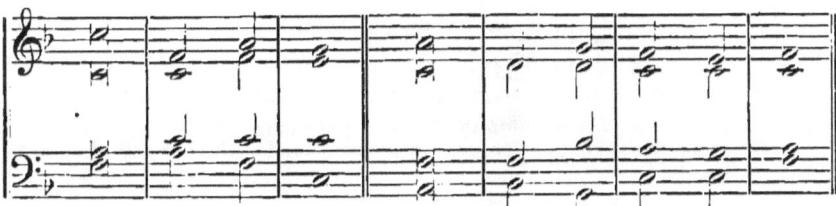

p GOD be merciful un-to | **us..and** | **bless us** : ||
And cause His face..to | **shine** — | **up-on** | **us.**
That Thy way may..be | **known..upon** | **earth** : ||
Thy sa-ving | **health..a-** | **mong..all** | **nations.**
f Let the people praise | **Thee,..O** | **God** : ||
Let | **all..the** | **peo-ple** | **praise Thee.**
O let the nations be glad..and | **sing..for** | **joy** : ||
For Thou shalt judge the people righteously, and govern..the | **na-tions** | **up-on** | **earth.**
ff Let the people praise | **Thee,..O** | **God** : ||
Let | **all..the** | **peo-ple** | **praise Thee.**
mf Then shall the earth | **yield..her** | **increase** : ||
And God, even our..own | **God,..shall** | **bless** — | **us.**
p God..shall | **bless** — | **us** :
And all the ends of..the | **earth..shall** | **fear** -- | **Him.**

PSALMS.

DEUS NOSTER REFUGIUM. Chant No. **XXXV**.

mf GOD..is our | refuge..and | strength : ‖
    A very pre-sent | help — | in — | trouble.

   Therefore will not we fear, though the earth | be re- | moved : ‖
   And though the mountains be car-ried into the | midst — | of..the | sea ;

ff Though the waters thereof roar | and..be | troubled : ‖
   Though the mountains shake | with..the | swelling..there- | of.

   There is a river, the streams whereof shall make glad..the | city..of | God : ‖
   The holy place of the tabernacles | of..the | Most — | High.

mf God is in the midst of her, she..shall | not..be | moved : ‖
   God shall help her,..and | that..right | ear- — | ly.

f The heathen raged, the king-doms were | mov- — | ed : ‖
   He uttered His voice,..the | earth — | melt- — | ed.

   The Lord of hosts..is | with — | us : ‖
   The God of Ja-cob | is — | our — | refuge.

   Come, behold the works | of..the | Lord : ‖
   What desolation He..hath | made — | in..the | earth.

p He maketh wars to cease..unto the end | of..the | earth : ‖
   He breaketh the bow, and cutteth the spear in sunder; he bur-neth the | cha-riot | in..the | fire.

pp Be still, and know..that | I..am | God : ‖
   I will be exalted among the heathen, I will..be ex- | alt-ed | in..the | earth.

mf The Lord..of | hosts..is | with us : ‖
   The God of Ja-cob | is — | our — | refuge.

MAGNUS DOMINUS. Chant No. **XXXVI**.

PSALMS.

f **GREAT** is the Lord, and great-ly | to..be | praised : ‖
In the city of our God, in the moun-tain | of..His | ho-li- | ness.

Beautiful for situation, the joy of the whole earth,..is | mount — | Zion : ‖
On the sides of the north, the city of the great King. God is known..in her | pala-ces | for..a | refuge.

For, lo, the kings | were..as- | sembled : ‖
They passed | by..to- | ge- — | ther.

They saw it, and | so..they | marvelled : ‖
They..were | troubled,..and | hasted..a- | way.

As we have heard, so have we seen in the city of the Lord of hosts, in the city | of..our | God : ‖
God..will establish | it..for- | ev- — | er.

MAGNUS DOMINUS. Second Part. Chant No. XXXVII.

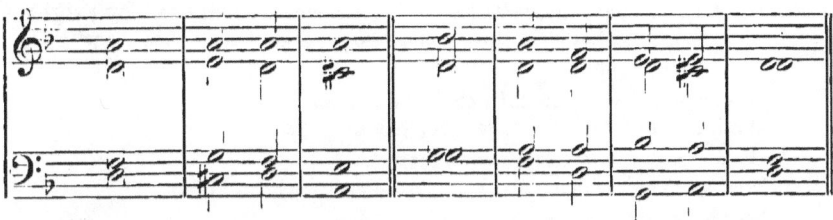

mf **WE** have thought of Thy loving-kind-ness, | O — | God : ‖
In..the | midst — | of..Thy | temple.

According to Thy name, O God, so is Thy praise..unto the | ends..of the | earth : ‖
Thy right hand..is | full..of | righ-teous- | ness.

f Let mount Zion rejoice, let the daugh-ters of | Judah..be | glad : ‖
Be- | cause — | of..Thy | judgments.

mf Walk about Zion, and..go | round..a- | bout her : ‖
Tell..the | tow-ers | there- — | of.

Mark ye well her bulwarks, con- | sider..her | palaces : ‖
That ye may tell..it to the | ge-ne- | ra-tion | following.

For this God is our God..for | ever..and | ever : ‖
He will be..our | guide..even | unto | death.

PSALMS.

MISERERE MEI. Chant No. XXXVIII.

p **H**AVE mercy upon me, O God, accord-ing to Thy | lov-ing- | kindness: ‖
According unto the multitude of Thy tender mer-cies blot | out — | my.. trans- | gressions.

Wash me thoroughly..from | mine..in- | iquity : ‖
And cleanse..me | from..my | sin.

For I acknow-ledge | my..trans- | gressions: ‖
And my sin..is | ever..be- | fore — | me.

Against Thee, Thee only, have I sinned, and done this e-vil | in..Thy | sight: ‖
That Thou mightest be justified when Thou speakest, and be clear | when — | Thou — | judgest.

Purge me with hyssop, and..I | shall..be | clean : ‖
Wash me, and I shall..be | whi-ter | than — | snow.

Make me to hear | joy..and | gladness: ‖
That the bones which Thou hast | bro-ken | may..re- | joice.

Hide Thy face | from..my | sins: ‖
And blot out all..of | mine..in- | i-qui- | ties.

Create in me..a clean | heart,..O | God: ‖
And renew..a right | spirit..with- | in — | me.

Cast me not away | from..Thy | presence: ‖
And take not Thy | Ho-ly | Spir-it | from me.

Restore unto me the joy..of | Thy..sal- | vation: ‖
And uphold..me | with..Thy | free — | Spirit.

f Then will I teach..trans- | gressors..Thy | ways: ‖
And sinners shall be..con- | vert-ed | un-to | Thee.

ff O Lord, o-pen | Thou..my | lips: ‖
And my mouth..shall show | forth — | Thy — | praise.

mf For Thou desi-rest not | sa-cri- | fice; ‖
Else would I give it: Thou delight-est | not..in | burnt- — | offering.

The sacrifices of God..are a | bro-ken | spirit: ‖
A broken and a contrite heart, O God, Thou | wilt — | not..des- | pise.

—68—

PSALMS.

QUI, HABITAT. Chant No. XXXIX.

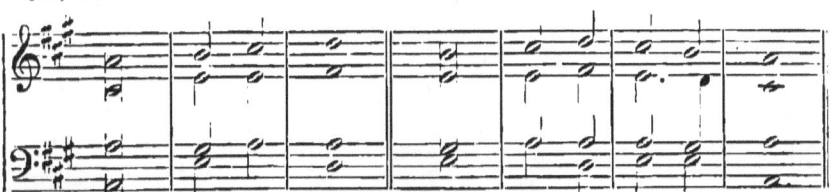

mf HE that dwelleth in the secret place..of the | Most — | High: ‖
Shall abide under the | shadow..of | the..Al- | mighty.
I will say of the Lord, He is my re-fuge | and..my | fortress: ‖
My God;..in | Him — | will..I | trust.
Surely He shall deliver thee from the snare | of..the | fowler: ‖
And from..the | noi-some | pes-ti- | lence.
He shall cover thee with His feathers, and under His wings | shalt..thou | trust: ‖
His truth..shall | be..thy | shield..and | buckler.
Thou shalt not be afraid for..the | terror..by | night: ‖
Nor for..the | arrow..that | flieth..by | day;
Nor for the pestilence that | walketh..in | darkness: ‖
Nor for the destruction that | wasteth..at | noon- — | day.
A thousand shall fall at thy side, and ten thou-sand at | thy..right | hand: ‖
But..it shall | not..come | nigh — | thee.

QUI, HABITAT. Second Part. Chant No. XL.

mf BECAUSE thou hast made the Lord..which | is..my | refuge: ‖
Even the Most High,..thy | ha-bi- | ta- — | tion;
There shall no e-vil be- | fall — | thee: ‖
Neither shall any plague..come | nigh..thy | dwell- — | ing.
For He shall give His angels charge | o-ver | thee: ‖
To keep..thee in | all — | thy — | ways.
They shall bear thee up | in..their | hands: ‖
Lest thou dash..thy | foot..a- | gainst..a | stone.
Thou shalt tread upon..the | lion..and | adder: ‖
The young lion and the dragon shalt..thou | tram-ple | un-der | feet.
Because he hath set his love upon me, therefore will I..de- | liv-er | him: ‖
I will set him on high, because | he..hath | known..my | Name.
mf He shall call upon me, and I..will | an-swer | him: ‖
I will be with him in trouble; I will deliv-er | him,..and | hon-or | him.
With long life..will I | satisfy | him: ‖
And..show | him — | my..sal- | vation.

PSALMS.

BONUM EST CONFITERI. Chant No. XLI.

f IT is a good thing to give thanks..un- | to..the | Lord : ‖
And to sing praises unto Thy | **Name**,..O | Most — | High ;
To show forth Thy loving-kind-ness | in..the | morning: ‖
And..Thy | **faithful-ness** | ev-ery | night,
ff Upon an instrument of ten strings, and..up- | on..the | lute : ‖
Upon..the | **harp..with a** | so-lemn | sound.
For Thou, Lord, hast made me glad | through..Thy | work : ‖
I will triumph in..the | **works —** | of..Thy | hands.

EXALTABO TE. Chant No. XLII.

f I WILL extol Thee,..my | God, O | King : ‖
And I will bless Thy Name..for- | **ev-er** | and — | ever.
Every day..will I | bless — | Thee : ‖
And I will praise Thy Name..for- | **ev-er** | and — | ever.
Great is the Lord, and great-ly to be | prais- — | ed : ‖
And His great-ness | **is..un-** | sear-cha- | ble.
One generation shall praise Thy works | to..a- | nother : ‖
And shall..de- | **clare..Thy** | migh-ty | acts.
I will speak of the glorious hon-or of Thy | ma-jes- | ty : ‖
And.. | **of..Thy** | won-drous | works.
And men shall speak of the might..of Thy | terri-ble | acts : ‖
And I will..de- | **clare..Thy** | great- — | ness.
They shall abundantly utter the mem-ory of | Thy..great | goodness : ‖
And..shall | **sing..of Thy** | righ-teous- | ness.

Second Part.

mf THE Lord is gra-cious, and | full of..com- | passion : ‖
Slow to anger, | **and..of** | great — | mercy.
The Lord..is | good..to | all : ‖
And His tender mer-cies are | **o-ver** | all..His | works.

—70—

PSALMS.

f All Thy works shall praise..Thee, | O — | Lord : ‖
  And..Thy | saints..shall | bless — | Thee.
They shall speak of the glo-ry | of..Thy | kingdom : ‖
  And | talk — | of..Thy | power ;
To make known to the sons of men..His | migh-ty | acts : ‖
  And the glo-rious | majes-ty | of..His | kingdom.
ff Thy kingdom is an ev-er- | last-ing | kingdom : ‖
  And Thy dominion endur-eth throughout | all — | ge-ne- | rations.
mf The Lord uphol-deth | all..that | fall : ‖
  And raiseth up..all | those..that be | bow-ed | down.
The eyes of all wait..up- | on — | Thee : ‖
  And Thou givest them..their | meat in..due | sea- — | son.
Thou o-penest | Thine — | hand : ‖
  And satisfiest the desire..of | ev-ery | liv-ing | thing.

Third Part.

mf THE Lord is righ-teous in | all..His | ways : ‖
  And ho-ly in | all — | His — | works.
The Lord is nigh unto all them that call..up- | on — | Him : ‖
  To all that call..up- | on — | Him..in | truth.
He will fulfil the desire of them..that | fear — | Him : ‖
  He also will hear..their | cry,..and will | save — | them.
The Lord preserveth all them..that | love — | Him : ‖
  But all..the | wicked..will | He..des- | troy.
ff My mouth shall speak the praise | of..the | Lord : ‖
  And let all flesh bless His ho-ly | Name..for- | ever..and | ever.

LEVAVI OCULOS.   Chant No. XLIII.

mf I WILL lift up mine eyes..un- | to..the | hills : ‖
  From | whence — | cometh..my | help.
My help co-meth | from..the | Lord : ‖ which | made — | heaven..and | earth.
He will not suffer thy foot | to..be | moved : ‖
  He..that | keepeth..thee | will..not | slumber.
Behold, He that keep-eth | Is-ra- | el : ‖ shall nei-ther | slum- — | ber..nor | sleep.
The Lord | is..thy | keeper : ‖ the Lord is thy shade..up- | on..thy | right — | hand.
The sun shall not smite.. | thee..by | day : ‖ nor..the | moon — | by — | night.
The Lord shall preserve..thee | from..all | evil : ‖ He..shall..pre- | serve..thy | soul.
The Lord shall preserve thy going out..and thy | com-ing | in : ‖
  From this time forth,..and | even..for- | ev-er- | more.

PSALMS.

MISERICORDIAS DOMINI. Chant No. XLIV.

f I WILL sing of the mer-cies of the | **Lord..for-** | **ever:** ‖
With my mouth will I make known Thy faithfulness | to..all | ge-ne- | rations.

mf For I have said, Mercy shall be built | **up..for-** | **ever:** ‖
Thy faithfulness shalt Thou establish | in..the | ver-y | heavens.

ff And the heavens shall praise Thy wonders, | **O —** | **Lord:** ‖
Thy faithfulness also in the con-gre- | ga-tion | of..the | saints.

mf For who in the heaven can be compa-red un- | **to..the** | **Lord?** ‖
Who among the sons of the might-y can be | likened..un- | to..the | Lord?

f God is greatly to be feared in the assem-bly | **of..the** | **saints:** ‖
And to be had in reverence of all | them..that | are..a- | bout **Him**.

Second Part.

f O LORD GOD of hosts, who is a strong Lord..like | **un-to** | **Thee?** ‖
Or to Thy faithfulness | round..a- | bout — | Thee?

Thou rulest the ra-ging | **of..the** | **sea:** ‖
When the waves thereof a- | rise,..Thou | still-est | them.

mf The heavens are Thine, the earth | **also..is** | **Thine:** ‖
As for the world, and the fulness thereof, | Thou..hast | found-ed | them.

Thou hast..a | **might-y** | **arm:** ‖
Strong is Thy hand, and high : | is..Thy | right — | hand.

Justice and judgment are the habita-tion | **of..Thy** | **throne:** ‖
Mercy and truth..shall | go..be- | fore..Thy | face.

f Blessed is the people that know..the | **joy-ful** | **sound:** ‖
They shall walk, O Lord,..in the | light of..Thy | coun-te- | nance.

In Thy Name shall they rejoice | **all..the** | **day:** ‖
And in Thy righteousness | shall..they | be..ex- | alted.

—72—

PSALMS.

For Thou art the glo-ry | of..their | strength: ||
And in Thy fav-or our | horn..shall | be..ex- | alted.

For the Lord..is | our..de- | fence: ||
And the Holy One..of | Is-rael | is..our | King.

ff Blessed be the Lord..for | ev-er- | more: ||
A..men | and — | A- — | men.

CONFITEBOR TIBI. Chant No. XLV.

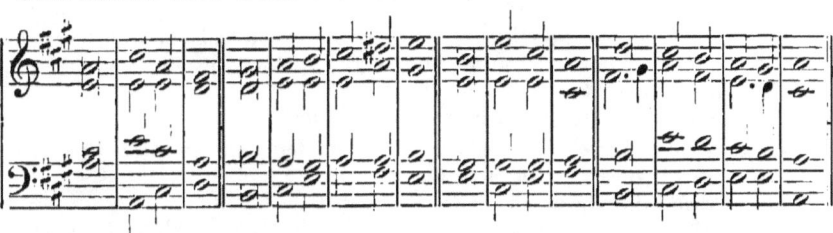

f I WILL praise..Thee with | my..whole | heart: ||
Before the gods will I sing | praise — | un-to | Thee.

I will worship toward Thy holy temple, and praise Thy Name for Thy loving-kind-ness and | for..Thy | truth: ||
For Thou hast magnified..Thy word a- | bove — | all Thy | Name.

In the day when I cried..Thou | answer-edst | me: ||
And strengthenedst me..with | strength — | in..my | soul.

ff All the kings of the earth..shall praise | Thee,..O | Lord: ||
When they hear..the | words — | of..Thy | mouth.

Yea, they shall sing in the ways | of..the | Lord: ||
For great..is the | glo-ry | of..the | Lord.

mf Though the Lord be high, yet hath He respect un- | to..the | lowly: ||
But the proud..He | know-eth a- | far — | off.

p Though I walk in the midst of trouble, Thou wilt..re- | vive — | me: ||
Thou shalt stretch forth Thine hand against the wrath of mine enemies, and Thy right | hand..shall | save — | me.

The Lord will perfect that..which con- | cern-eth | me: ||
Thy mercy, O Lord, endureth forever; forsake not the works..of | Thine — | own — | hands.

—73—

PSALMS.

DOMINE REFUGIUM. Chant No. XLVI.

mf LORD, Thou hast been..our | dwell-ing- | place: ||
In | all — | ge-ne- | rations.
                                                                 [and..the | world: ||
Before the mountains were brought forth, or ever Thou hadst formed the earth|
Even from everlasting to ev-er- | last-ing, | Thou..art | God.

Thou turnest man | to..des- | truction: ||
And sayest, Return,..ye | chil-dren | of — | men.

For a thousand years in Thy sight are but as yesterday..when | it..is | past: ||
And as..a | watch — | in..the | night.

Thou carriest them away..as | with..a | flood; ||
                                                                  [up.
They are as a sleep: in the morning they are..like|grass..which|grow-eth

In the morning it flourisheth, and | grow-eth | up: ||
In the eve-ning it is cut | down,..and | wi-ther- | eth.

For we are consu-med | by..Thine | anger: ||
And by..Thy | wrath — | are..we | troubled.

Thou hast set our iniquities..be- | fore — | Thee : ||
Our secret sins..in the | light of..Thy | coun-te- | nance.

For all our days are passed away | in..Thy | wrath : ||
We spend our years,..as a | tale — | that..is | told.

The days of our years are threescore years and ten; and if by reason of strength..
they be | four-score | years: ||
                                                                   [a- | way.
Yet is their strength labor and sorrow; for it is soon cut off,..and|we — | fly.

Who knoweth the power | of..Thine | anger? ||
Even accord-ing to Thy | fear,..so | is..Thy | wrath.

So teach us..to | number..our | days: || ·
That we may apply..our | hearts — | un-to | wisdom.

Return...O | Lord,..how | long? ||
And let it repent Thee..con- | cerning..Thy | ser- — | vants.

O satisfy us ear-ly | with..Thy | mercy: ||
That we may rejoice and..be | glad — | all..our | days.

Make us glad according to the days wherein Thou hast..af- | flict-ed | us: ||
And the years..where- | in..we | have..seen | evil.

Let Thy work appear..un- | to..Thy | servants: ||
And..Thy | glory..un- | to..their | children.

And let the beauty of the Lord our God be..up- | on — | us: ||
And establish Thou the work of our hands upon us; yea, the work of our
hands..e- | stab-lish | Thou — | it.

—74—

PSALMS.

JUBILATE DEO. Chant No. XLVII.

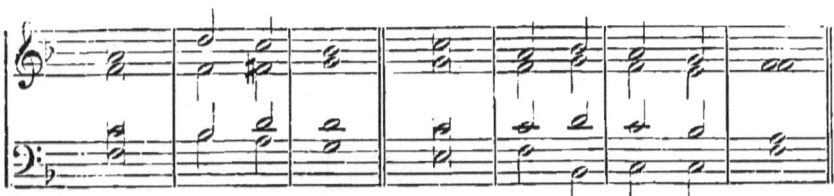

f **M**AKE a joyful noise unto the Lord, | **all..ye** | **lands:** ||
    Serve the Lord with gladness; come before..His | **pre-sence** | **with —** | singing.

Know ye that the Lord | **He..is** | **God;** ||
    It is He that hath made us, and not we ourselves: we are His peo-ple, and the | **sheep —** | **of..His** | **pasture.**

ff Enter into His gates with thanksgiving, and into His | **courts..with** | **praise:** ||
    Be thankful un-to | **Him,..and** | **bless..His** | **Name.**

For the Lord is good; His mer-cy is | **ev-er-** | **lasting:** ||
    And His truth endur-eth to | **all —** | **ge-ne-** | **rations.**

VENITE EXULTEMUS DOMINO. Chant No. XLVIII.

f O COME, let us sing..un- | **to..the** | **Lord:** ||
    Let us make a joyful noise..to the | **rock..of** | **our..sal-** | **vation.**

Let us come before His pre-sence | **with..thanks-** | **giving:** ||
    And make a joyful noise..unto | **Him —** | **with —** | **psalms.**

For the Lord..is a | **great —** | **God:** ||
    And a great | **King..a-** | **bove..all** | **gods.**

In His hand are the deep pla-ces | **of..the** | **earth:** ||
    The strength of the hills..is | **His —** | **al- —** | **so.**

The sea is His, | **and..He** | **made it:** ||
    And His hands | **formed..the** | **dry —** | **land.**

ff O come, let us wor-ship | **and..bow** | **down:** ||
    Let us kneel..be- | **fore..the** | **Lord..our** | **Maker.**

For..He | **is..our** | **God:** ||
    And we are the people of His pas-ture and the | **sheep —** | **of..His** | **hand.**

PSALMS.

CONFITEMINI DOMINI. Chant No. XLIX.

f O GIVE thanks unto the Lord, for | He..is | good: ‖
　　Because..His | mercy..en- | dureth..for- | ever.

　　Let them now that fear..the | Lord — | say: ‖
　　That..His | mercy..en- | dureth..for- | ever.

　　The Lord is my | strength..and | song: ‖ and is..be- | come — | my..sal- | vation.

　　The voice of rejoicing and salvation is in the tabernacles | of..the | righteous: ‖
　　The right hand of..the | Lord..doeth | va-liant- | ly.

　　The right hand of the Lord | is..ex- | alted: ‖
　　The right hand of..the | Lord — | do-eth | valiantly.

mf I shall..not | die,..but | live: ‖ and declare..the | works — | of..the | Lord.

　　The Lord..hath | chastened..me | sore: ‖
　　But He hath not given me | o-ver | un-to | death.

f Open to me the gates..of | right-eous- | ness: ‖
　　I will go into them,..and | I..will | praise..the | Lord;

　　This gate | of..the | Lord: ‖ into which..the | right-eous | shall — | enter.

　　I will praise Thee, for Thou..hast | heard — | me: ‖
　　And art..be- | come — | my..sal- | vation.

mf The stone which the | builders..re- | fused: ‖
　　Is become..the | head..stone | of..the | corner.

　　This is..the | Lord's — | doing: ‖ it..is | marvel-lous | in..our | eyes.

　　This is the day which the | Lord..hath | made: ‖
　　We will..re- | joice..and | be..glad | in it.

　　Save now,..I be- | seech Thee,..O | Lord: ‖
　　O Lord, I beseech Thee,..send | now..pros- | per-i- | ty.

　　Blessed be he that cometh in the Name | of..the | Lord: ‖
　　We have blessed you out..of the | house — | of..the | Lord.

　　God is the Lord,..which hath | showed..us | light: ‖
　　Bind the sacrifice with cords, even unto the | horns — | of..the | altar.

f Thou art my God, and I..will | praise — | Thee: ‖
　　Thou art my God,..I | will..ex- | alt — | Thee.

ff O give thanks..un- | to..the | Lord: ‖
　　For He is good: for..His | mercy..en- | dureth..for- | ever.

PSALMS.

CONFITEMINI DOMINO IN AETERNUM. Chant No. L.

f O GIVE thanks..un- | to..the | Lord ; ||
　　For He is good: for..His | mercy..en- | dureth..for- | ever.

　O give thanks..unto the | God..of | gods: ||
　　For..His | mercy..en- | dureth..for- | ever.

　O give thanks..to the | Lord..of | lords: ||
　　For..His | mercy..en- | dureth..for- | ever.

mf To Him who alone | doeth..great | wonders: ||
　　For..His | mercy..en- | dureth..for- | ever.

　To Him that by wis-dom | made..the | heavens: ||
　　For..His | mercy..en- | dureth..for- | ever.

　To Him that stretched out the earth..a- | bove..the | waters: ||
　　For..His | mercy..en- | dureth..for- | ever.

　To Him..that | made..great | lights: ||
　　For..His | mercy..en- | dureth..for- | ever.

　Who remembered us..in our | low..es- | tate: ||
　　For..His | mercy..en- | dureth..for- | ever.

　And hath redeemed us from..our | en-e- | mies: ||
　　For..His | mercy..en- | dureth..for- | ever.

　Who giv-eth | food..to all | flesh: ||
　　For..His | mercy..en- | dureth..for- | ever.

f O give thanks unto the | God..of | heaven: ||
　　For..His | mercy..en- | dureth..for- | ever.

PSALMS.

DOMINE DOMINUS NOSTER. Chant No. LI.

f **O** LORD our Lord, how excellent is Thy Name..in | all..the | earth : ||
Who hast set..Thy | glory..a- | bove..the | heavens.

Out of the mouth of babes and sucklings hast Thou ordained strength..because | of..Thine | enemies : ||
That Thou mightest still the enemy | and — | the..a- | venger.

mf When I consider Thy heavens, the work | of..Thy | fingers : ||
The moon and the stars, | which..Thou | hast..or- | dained ;

What is man, that Thou..art | mindful..of | him ? ||
And the son of man, | that..Thou | visit-est | him ?

For Thou hast made him a little low-er | than..the | angels : ||
And hast crowned him..with | glory..and | hon- — | or.

Thou madest him to have dominion over the works | of..Thy | hands : ||
Thou hast put..all | things..un- | der..his | feet.

ff O.. | Lord..our | Lord : || how excellent is Thy | Name..in | all..the | earth !

CANTATE DOMINO. Chant No. LII.

f **O** SING unto the Lord..a | new — | song : ||
For He hath | done — | marvel-lous | things.

His right hand,..and His | ho-ly | arm : ||
Hath..gotten | Him..the | vic-tor- | y.

PSALMS.

The Lord hath made known | His..sal- | vation: ‖
His righteousness hath He openly showed..in the | sight — | of..the | heathen.

He hath remembered His mercy and His truth toward..the | house..of | Israel: ‖
All the ends of the earth have seen..the sal- | vation | of..our | God.

ff Make a joyful noise unto the Lord, | all..the | earth: ‖
Make a loud noise, and re- | joice, — | and..sing | praise.

Sing unto the Lord | with..the | harp: ‖
With the harp,..and the | voice — | of..a | psalm.

mf Let the floods clap their hands; let the hills be joyful together..be- | fore..the |
For He cometh..to | judge — | the — | earth ;   [Lord : ‖

With righteousness shall..He | judge..the | world : ‖
And..the | people..with | e-qui- | ty.

DE PROFUNDIS. Chant No. LIII.

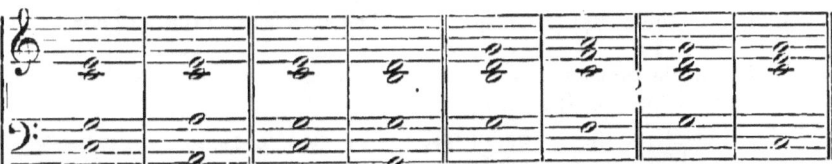

pp OUT of the depths have..I.. | cried: ‖
Unto Thee, O.. | Lord. ‖

Lord, hear..my.. | voice: ‖
Let Thine ears be attentive to the voice..of my..suppli- | cations. ‖

If Thou, Lord, shouldst mark..iniqui- | ties: ‖
O Lord,..who shall | stand? ‖

But there is forgiveness..with | Thee: ‖
That Thou mayest..be | feared. ‖

I wait for the Lord, my soul..doth | wait: ‖
And in His word..do I | hope. ‖

My soul waiteth for the Lord more than they that watch..for the | morning: ‖
I say, more than they that watch..for the | morning. ‖

Let Israel hope in the Lord, for with the Lord..there is | mercy : ‖
And with Him is plenteous..re- | demption. ‖

And He shall redeem..Is- | rael: ‖
From all his iniqui- | ties. ‖

PSALMS.

TE DECET HYMNUS. Chant No LIV.

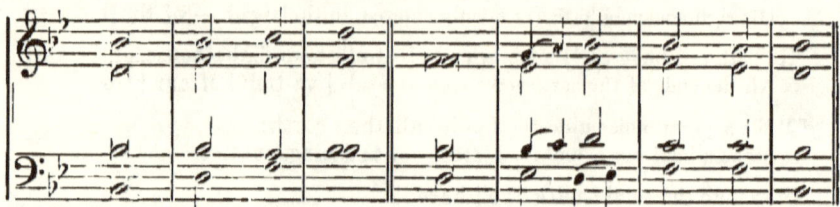

mf PRAISE waiteth for Thee,..O | God,..in | Sion: ‖
And unto Thee shall..the | vow..be per- | form- — | ed.

O Thou..that | hear-est | prayer: ‖ unto Thee..shall | all — | flesh — | come.

Blessed is the man whom Thou choosest, and causest to approach unto Thee,
that he may dwell | in..Thy | courts: ‖   [temple.
We shall be satisfied with the goodness of Thy house, ev-en | of..Thy | ho-ly |

By terrible things in righteousness wilt Thou answer us, O God..of | our..sal- | vation: ‖
Who art the confidence of all the ends of the earth, and of them that are..a- | far..off up- | on..the | sea;

Which by His strength setteth | fast..the | mountains: ‖
Being | gird- — | ed..with | power:

Which stilleth the noise | of..the | seas: ‖
The noise of their waves, and..the | tu-mult | of..the | people.

They also that dwell in the uttermost parts are afraid | at..Thy | tokens: ‖
Thou makest the out-goings of the morn-ing and | even-ing | to..re- | joice.

Thou visitest the earth,..and | water-est | it: ‖
Thou preparest them corn, when thou..hast | so..pro- | vid-ed | for it.

Thou waterest the ridges thereof..a- | bun-dant- | ly: ‖
Thou settlest..the | fur-rows | there- — | of.

Thou mak-est it | soft..with | showers: ‖
Thou blessest..the | spring-ing | there- — | of.

Thou crownest the year | with..Thy | goodness: ‖
And..Thy | paths — | drop — | fatness.

They drop upon the pas-tures of the | wil-der- | ness: ‖
And the little hills..re- | joice..on | ev-ery | side.

The pas-tures are | clothed..with | flocks: ‖
The valleys also are covered over with corn; they shout..for | joy,..they | al-so | sing.

PSALMS.

CONFITEBOR TIBI. Chant No. LV.

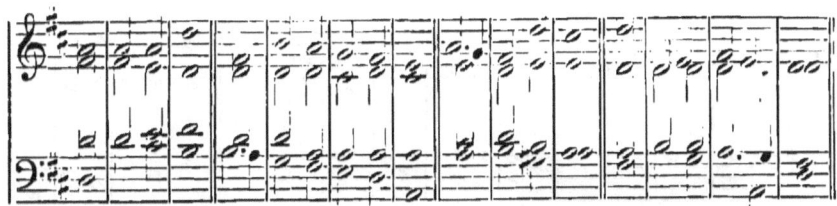

f PRAISE ye the Lord. I will praise the Lord..with | my..whole | heart: ‖
   In the assembly of the upright,..and | in..the | con-gre- | gation.

The works..of the | Lord..are | great: ‖
   Sought out of all them..that have | pleas-ure | there- — | in.

His work is honorable | and — | glorious: ‖
   And His righteousness en- | dureth..for- | ev- — | er.

He hath made His wonderful works..to | be..re- | membered: ‖
   The Lord is gra-cious and | full — | of..com- | passion.

He hath given meat unto them..that | fear — | Him: ‖
   He will ever be | mind-ful | of..His | covenant.

He hath showed His people the pow-er | of..His | works: ‖
   That He may give them..the | herit-age | of..the | heathen.

The works of His hands are verity..and | judg- — | ment: ‖
   All.. | His..com- | mandments..are | sure.

They stand fast..for- | ever..and | ever: ‖
   And are done..in | truth..and | up-right- | ness.

p He sent redemp-tion un- | to..His | people: ‖
   He hath commanded His covenant forever; ho-ly and | rev-erend |
   is..His | Name.

f The fear of the Lord is the be- | ginning..of | wisdom: ‖
   His.. | praise..en- | dureth..for- | ever.

Glory be to the Fath-er, and | to the | Son, ‖
   And.. | to the | Ho-ly | Ghost:

As it was in the beginning, is now, and | ever..shall | be, ‖
   World | with-out | end. A- | men.

PSALMS.

LAUDATE DOMINUM DE COELIS. Chant No. LVI.

f PRAISE ye the Lord: praise ye the Lord | from..the | heavens: ‖
    Praise..Him | in — | the — | heights. ‖
Praise ye Him, | all..His | angels: ‖
    Praise..ye | Him,— | all..His | hosts. ‖

Praise ye Him, | sun..and | moon: ‖
    Praise..Him, | all..ye | stars..of | light. ‖
Praise Him, ye | heavens..of | heavens: ‖
    And ye waters..that | be..a- | bove..the | heavens. ‖

Let them praise the Name | of..the | Lord: ‖
    For He command-ed, | and..they | were..cre- | ated. ‖
mf He hath also established them..for- | ever..and | ever: ‖
    He hath made..a de- | cree..which | shall..not | pass. ‖

ff Praise the Lord | from..the | earth: ‖
    Ye | drag-ons | and..all | deeps. ‖
Fire, and hail; | snow,..and | vapors: ‖
    Storm-y | wind..ful- | filling..His | word. ‖

Moun-tains, | and..all | hills: ‖
    Fruitful trees, | and — | all — | cedars; ‖
Beasts, | and..all | cattle: ‖
    Creeping things, | and — | fly-ing | fowl; ‖

Kings of the earth, | and..all | people: ‖
    Princes, and..all | judg-es | of..the | earth; ‖
Both..young | men,..and | maidens: ‖
    Old men, | and — | child- — | ren; ‖

Let them praise the Name | of..the | Lord: ‖
    For His Name alone is excellent; His glory is..a- | bove..the | earth..and | heaven. ‖
He also exalteth the horn of His people, the praise..of | all..His | saints: ‖
    Even of the children of Israel, a people near unto Him. | Praise — | ye..the | Lord. ‖

PSALMS.

DOMINI EST TERRA. Chant No. LVII.

mf THE earth is the Lord's, and..the | fulness..there- | of: ‖
　　The world,..and | they..that | dwell..there- | in.
　For He hath founded it..up- | on..the | seas : ‖
　And established | it..up- | on..the | floods.
mf Who shall ascend into the hill | of..the | Lord ? ‖
　And who shall stand | in..His | ho-ly | place ?
　He that hath clean hands, and..a | pure — | heart : ‖
　Who hath not lifted up his soul unto vanity,..nor | sworn..de- | ceit-ful- | ly.
　He shall receive the bless-ing | from..the | Lord : ‖
　And righteousness from..the | God..of | his..sal- | vation.
　This is the generation of | them..that | seek Him : ‖
　That.. | seek..thy | face,..O | Jacob.
ff Lift up your heads, | O..ye | gates ; ‖　　　　　　　　　　[come | in.
　And be ye lift up, ye everlasting doors : and the King..of | glo-ry | shall..
　Who is..this | King..of | glory ? ‖
　The Lord strong and mighty, the | Lord — | mighty..in | battle.
　Lift up your heads, | O..ye | gates ; ‖　　　　　　　　　　[come | in.
　Even lift them up, ye everlasting doors : and the King..of | glo-ry | shall..
　Who is..this | King..of | glory ? ‖
　The Lord of Hosts,..He | is..the | King..of | glory.

COELI ENARRANT. Chant No. LVIII.

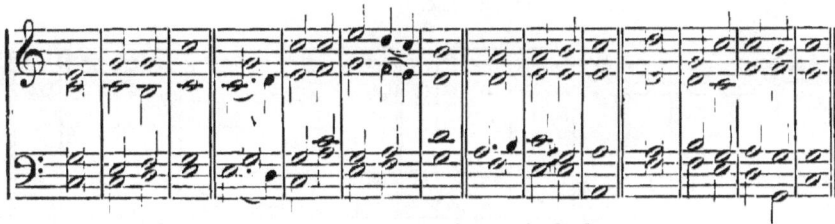

ff THE heavens declare..the | glory..of | God : ‖
　　And the firmament | showeth..His | hand-y | work.
mf Day unto day | utter-eth | speech : ‖
　And night unto | night — | show-eth | knowledge.
　There is..no | speech..nor | language : ‖
　Where..their | voice..is | not — | heard.
　Their line is gone out..through | all..the | earth : ‖
　And their words..to the | end — | of..the | world.

PSALMS.

COELI ENARRANT. Second Part. Chant No. LIX.

mf **T**HE law of the Lord is perfect, con- | verting..the | soul: ‖
    The testimony of the Lord is sure, | mak-ing | wise..the | simple.
The statutes of the Lord are right, re- | joicing..the | heart: ‖
    The commandment of the Lord..is | pure,..en- | lightening..the | eyes.
The fear of the Lord is clean,..en- | during..for- | ever: ‖
    The judgments of the Lord are true..and | right-eous | al-to- | gether.
More to be desired are they than gold, yea,..than | much..fine | gold: ‖
    Sweeter also than hon-ey | and..the | hon-ey- | comb.
Moreover, by them,..is Thy | ser-vant | warned: ‖
    And in keeping of them | there..is | great..re- | ward.

Third Part.

mf **W**HO can un-der- | stand..His | errors? ‖
    Cleanse Thou me | from — | se-cret | faults.
Keep back Thy servant also from..pre- | sump-tuous | sins; ‖
    Let them not have dominion over me: then shall I be upright, and I shall
      be innocent | from..the | great..trans- | gression.
Let the words of my mouth, and the medita-tion | of..my | heart: ‖
    Be acceptable in Thy sight, O Lord,..my | strength,..and | my..re- | deemer.

DOMINUS REGIT ME. Chant No. LX.

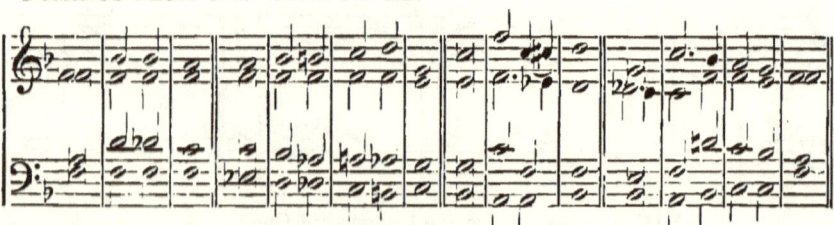

mf **T**HE Lord | is..my | shepherd: ‖ I | shall — | not — | want.
    He maketh me to lie down..in | green — | pastures: ‖
    He leadeth me..be- | side..the | still — | waters.
He..res- | toreth..my | soul: ‖
    He leadeth me in the paths of right-eous- | ness..for | His..Name's | sake.

PSALMS.

Yea, though I walk through the valley of the shadow of death, I..will | **fear..
no** | **evil:** ||
   For Thou art with me; Thy rod and Thy | **staff..they** | **com-fort** | **me.**

Thou preparest a table before me in the pres-ence | **of..mine** | **enemies:** ||
   Thou anointest my head with oil; my | **cup —** | **run-neth** | **over.**

Surely goodness and mercy shall follow me all..the | **days of..my** | **life:** ||
   And I will dwell..in the house | **of..the** | **Lord..for-** | **ever.**

IN CONVERTENDO. Chant No. LXI.

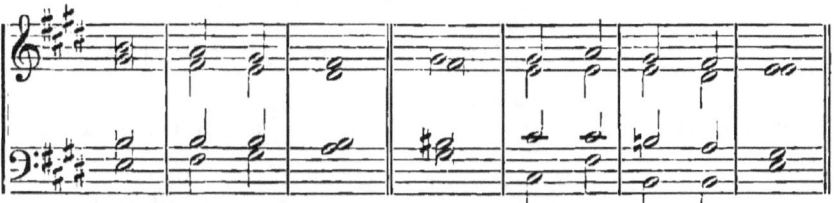

mf WHEN the Lord turned again the captivity | **of —** | **Zion:** ||
   We were like | **them —** | **that —** | **dream.**

Then was our mouth | **filled..with** | **laughter:** ||
   And..our | **tongue..with** | **sing- —** | **ing;**

Then said they..a- | **mong..the** | **heathen:** ||
   The Lord..hath | **done..great** | **things..for** | **them.**

The Lord hath done..great | **things..for** | **us:** ||
   Where- | **of —** | **we..are** | **glad.**

Turn again our captivity, | **O —** | **Lord:** ||
   As..the | **streams —** | **in..the** | **south.**

They..that | **sow..in** | **tears:** || shall | **reap —** | **in —** | **joy.**

He that goeth forth and weepeth, bear-ing | **pre-cious** | **seed:** ||
   Shall doubtless come again with rejoicing, | **bringing..his** | **sheaves..with** | **him.**

Glory be to the Fath-er, | **and..to the** | **Son,** ||
   And | **to..the** | **Ho-ly** | **Ghost:**

As it was in the beginning, is now, and | **ever..shall** | **be,** ||
   World | **with-out** | **end. A-** | **men.**

CHANT.

CANTEMUS CUNCTI. Chant No. LXII.

THE strain upraise of joy and praise, Alle- | lu- — | ia.
   To the glory of their King
Shall the ransomed | **people** | **sing,** || Alle- | lu- — | ia, || Alle- | lu- | ia.

And the choirs that | **dwell on** | **high**
Shall re-echo | **through the** | **sky,** || Alle- | lu- — | ia, || Alle- | lu- | ia.

They through the fields of | **Paradise that** | **roam,** ||
The blessed ones, repeat through | **that bright** | **home,** || Alle- | lu- — | ia, || Alle- | lu- | ia.

The planets glittering on their | **heavenly** | **way,** ||
The shining constellations, | **join and** | **say,** || Alle- | lu- — |ia, || Alle- | lu- | ia.

Ye clouds that onward sweep,
  Ye winds, on | **pinions** | **light,** ||
Ye thunders, echoing loud and deep,
  Ye lightnings, | **wildly** | **bright,** ||
In sweet con- | **sent u-** | **nite** || your Alle- | lu- | ia.

Ye floods and ocean billows,
  Ye storms and | **winter** | **snow,** ||
Ye days of cloudless beauty,
  Hoar-frost and | **summer** | **glow,** ||
Ye groves that wave in spring,
And glorious | **forests,** | **sing,** || Alle- | lu- | ia.

First let the birds, with painted | **plumage** | **gay,** ||
Exalt their great Creator's | **praise, and** | **say,** || Alle- | lu- — | ia, || Alle- | lu- | ia.

Then let the beasts of the earth with | **varying** | **strain,** ||
Join in Creation's Hymn, and | **cry a-** | **gain,** || Alle- | lu- — |ia, || Alle- | lu- |ia.

Here let the mountains thunder forth so- | **nor-** — | **ous,** || Alle- | lu- — | ia.
There let the valleys sing in gentler | **chor-** — | **us,** || Alle- | lu- | ia.

CHANT.

Thou jubilant abyss of | **ocean,** | **cry,** || Alle- | **lu-** — | **ia.**
Ye tracts of earth and conti- | **nents re-** | **ply,** || Alle- | **lu-** | **ia.**

To God, who all cre- | **ation** | **made,** ||
The frequent hymn be | **duly** | **paid:** || Alle- | **lu-** — | **ia,** || Alle- | **lu-** | **ia.**

This is the strain, the eternal strain, the Lord of | **all things** | **loves:** ||
   Alle- | **lu-** — | **ia.**
This is the song, the heavenly song, that Christ Him- | **self ap-** | **proves:** ||
   Alle- | **lu-** | **ia.**

Wherefore we sing, both heart and voice a- | **wak-** — | **ing,** || Alle- | **lu-** — | **ia.**
And children's voices echo, answer | **mak-** — | **ing,** || Alle- | **lu-** | **ia.**

Now from all men | **be out-** | **poured** ||
Alleluia | **to the** | **Lord;** ||
With Alleluia | **ever-** | **more** ||
The Son and Spirit | **we a-** | **dore.**

Praise be done to the | **Three in** | **One.** ||
Alle- | **lu-** — | **ia!** || Alleluia! Alle- | **lu-** — | **ia!** ||
   Alle- | **lu-** | **ia!** || **Amen.**

Metrical Tunes.

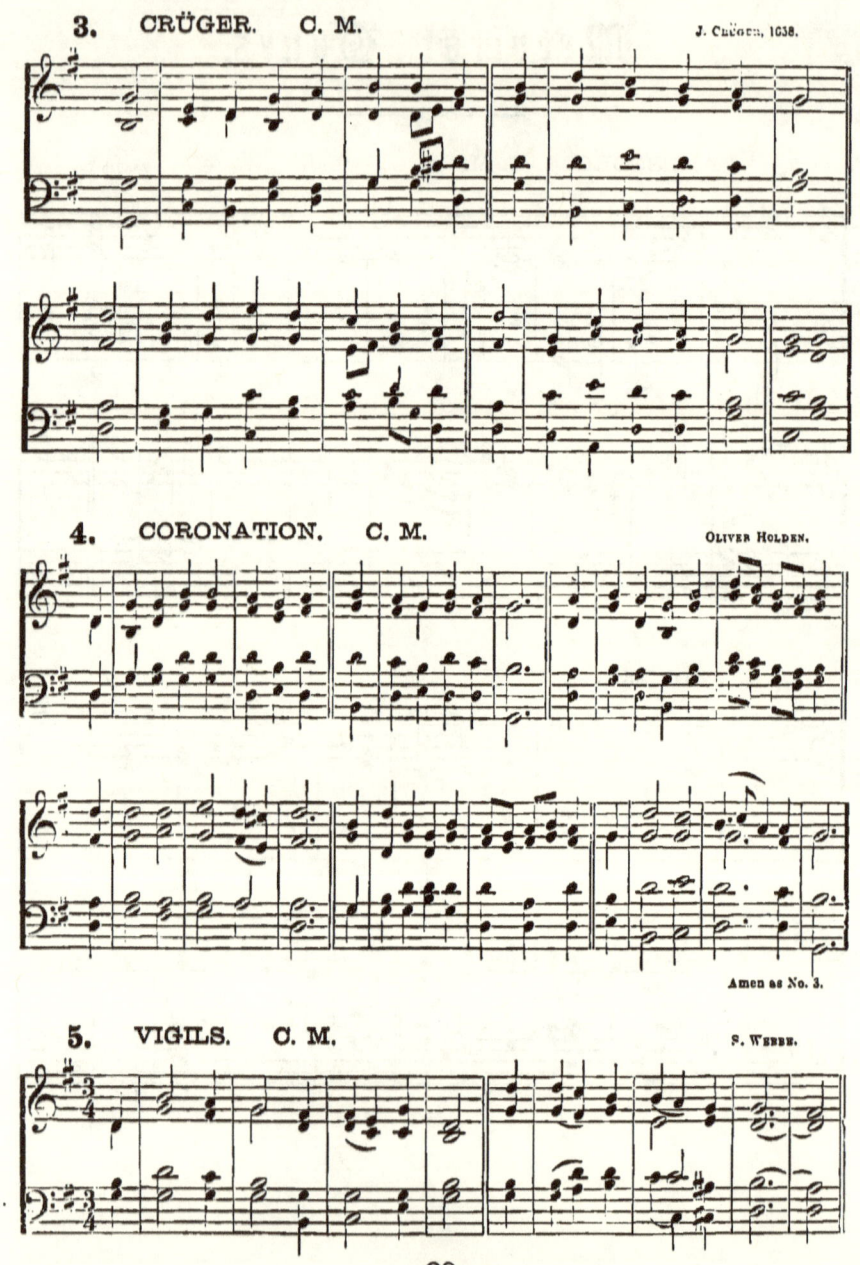

6. CHESTERFIELD. C. M. — Dr. Haweis.

7. ST. AGNES. C. M. — Rev. Dr. Dykes.

11. ST. ANN'S. C. M. — Dr. Croft, 1711.

12. KNECHT. C. M. — J. A. Knecht, 1793.

16. SOUTHWELL. C. M. — English Psalter, 1592.

17. HAWLEY. C. M. — A. R. Reinagle.

21. LOB GOTT. C. M. — Nicolas Hermann, 1560.

22. JERUSALEM. C. M. — Rev. Dr. Tucker's Hymnal.

26. WINDSOR.   C. M. (*Minor.*)   Kirby.

27. INVITATION.   C. M.   Unknown.

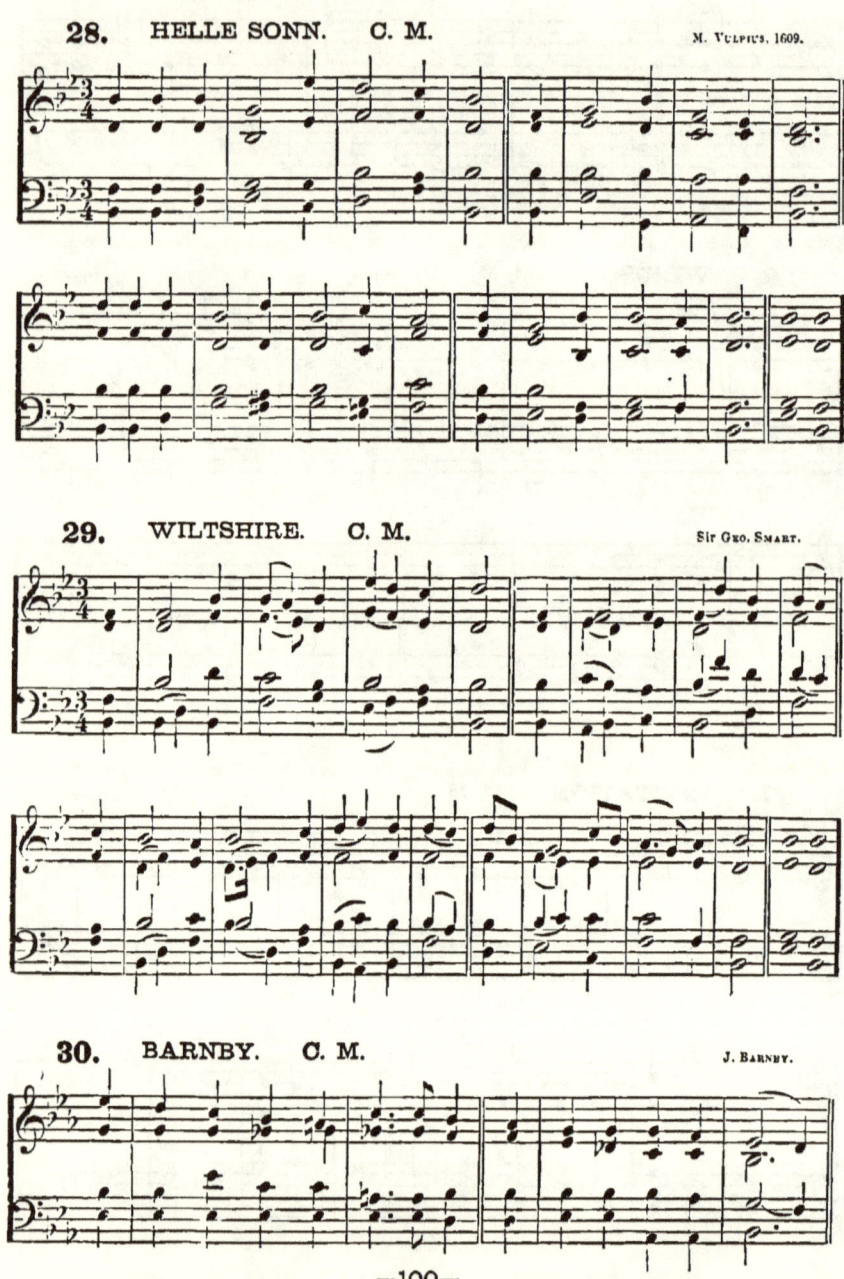

31. BEDFORD. C. M. 　　　　　W. WHEALL, 1669.

32. BELGRAVE. C. M. 　　　　　WM. HORSLEY.

36. ST. FRANCIS. C. M. G. A. LÖHR.

37. CHRISTMAS. C. M. From G. F. HANDEL.

Amen as No. 36.

41. MOREDON. C. M. R. Haking.

42. PALESTINE. C. M. J. Summers.

45. LOWESTOFFE. C. M. D.

Day's Psalter, 1569.

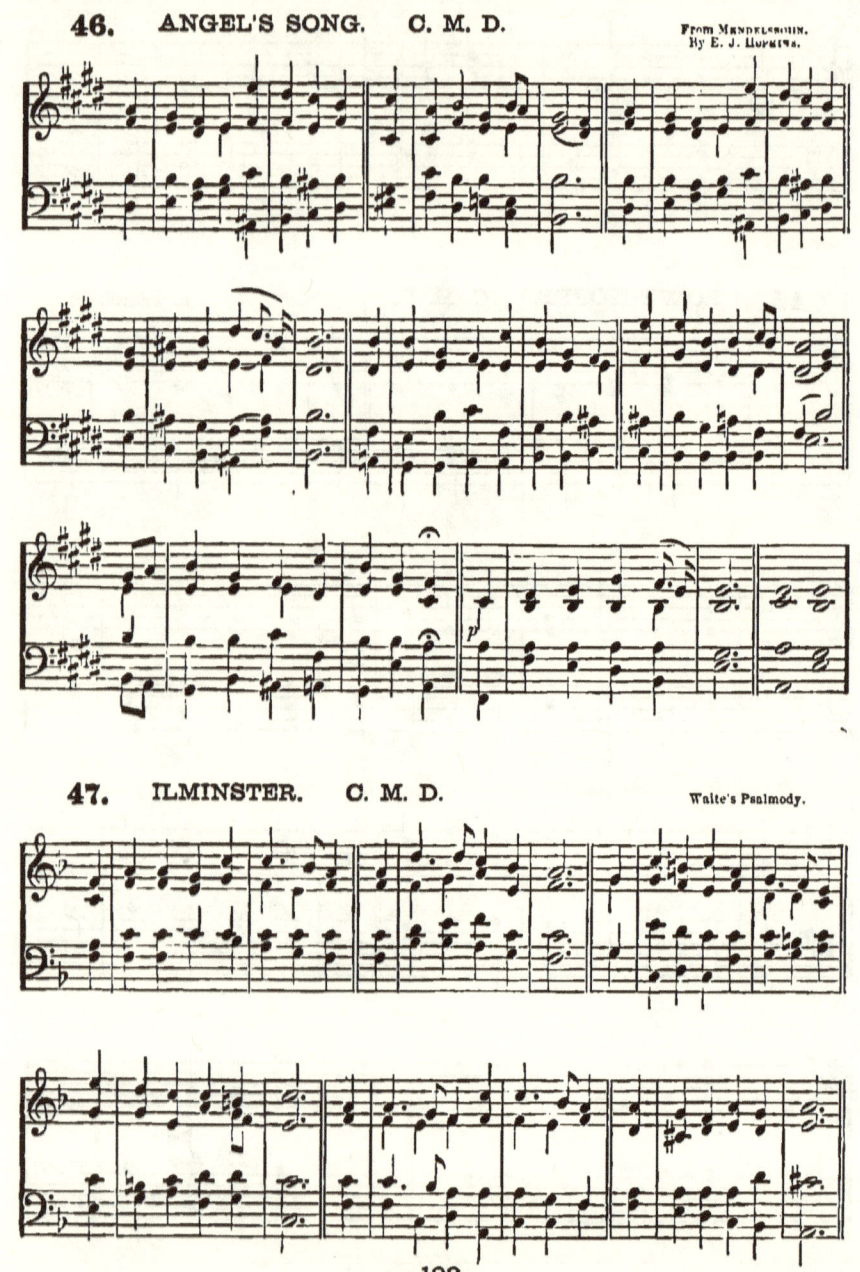

48. BRATTLE STREET.   C. M. D.   Ignaz Pleyel.

57. OLNEY. S. M. Dr. L. Mason.

58. DENNIS. S. M. H. G. Nägeli.

8   113—

67. OLD 25th. S. M. D.   Day's Psalter, 1563.

68. FAIRFIELD. S. M. D. Rev. P. Latrobe.

69. THESSALONICA. S. M. D. German, arr. by Goss.

70. KANE. S. M. D. Dr. L. Mason, harm. by Dibdin.

73. LENTZ. L. M.   Dr. Mainzer.

74. WINCHESTER. L. M.   From Cranselius, 1650.

83. STELLA L. M.   From "Crown of Jesus."

84. TRURO. L. M.   Dr. C. Burney, 17—.

87. MIGDOL. L. M. — Dr. L. Mason.

88. DEVOTION L. M. (*Peculiar.*) — From Goodrich & Gilbert's "Hymnal."

91. FEDERAL STREET. L. M.
H. K. Oliver.

92. HAMBURG. L. M.
Adapted by Dr. L. Mason.

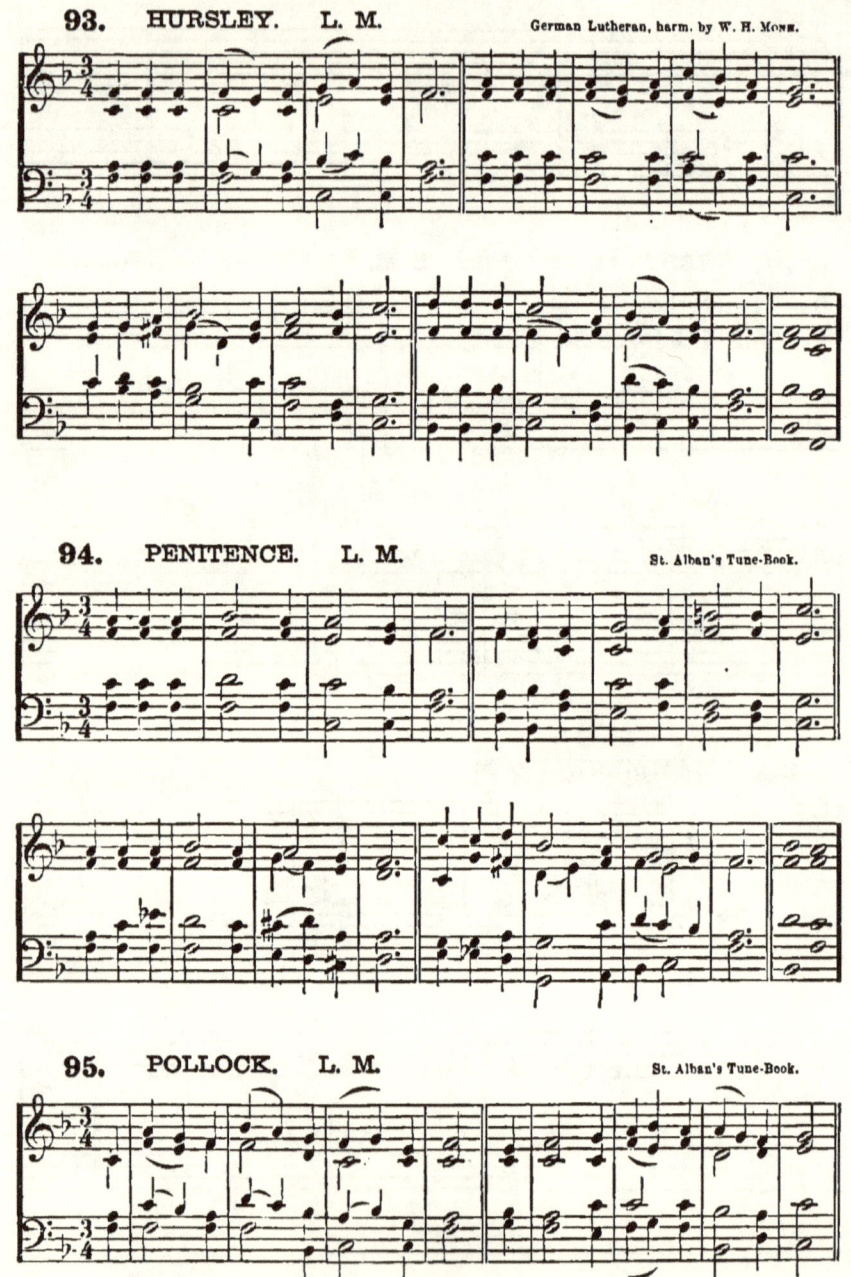

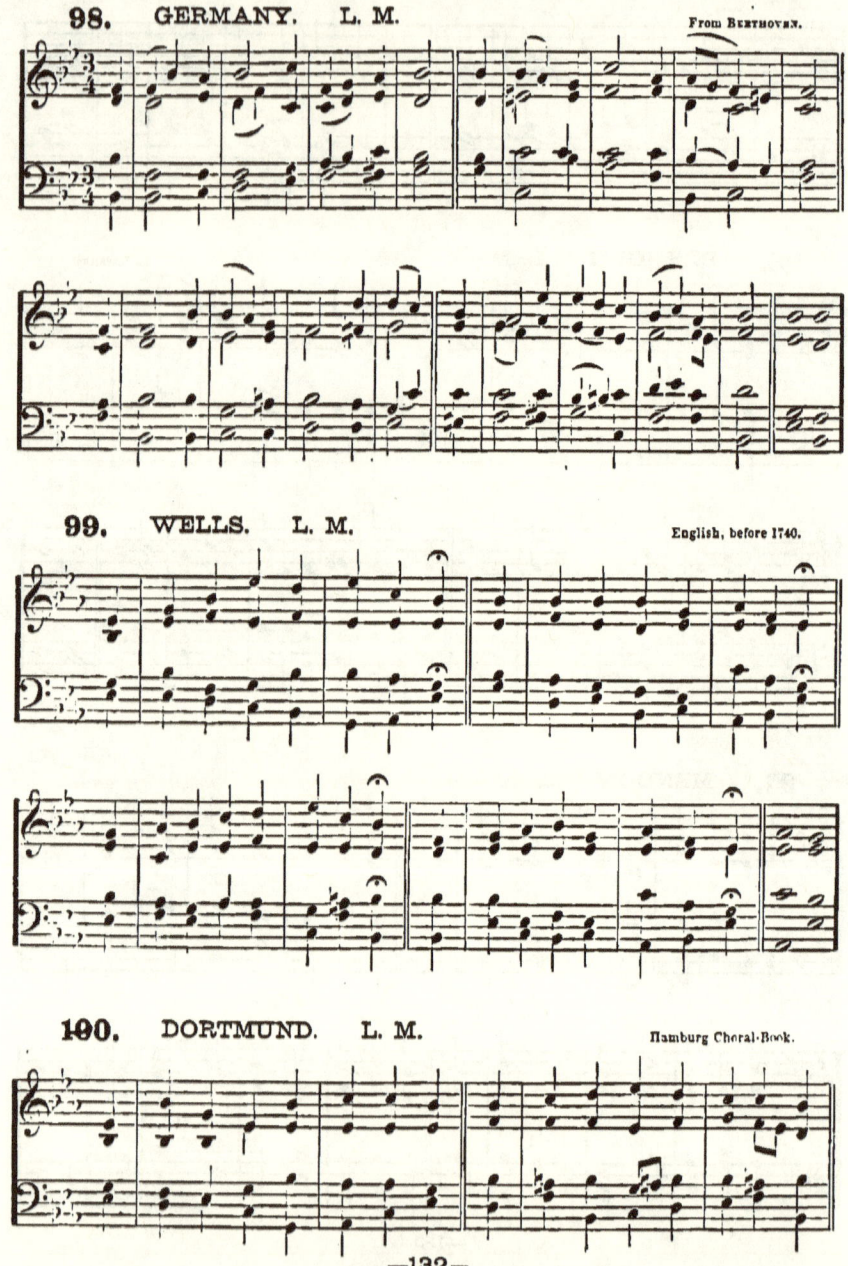

101. BONN. L. M. — Adapted by Goss.

102. VESPERS. L. M. — W. H. Hart.

105. CREATION. L. M. 6 lines. F. J. Haydn.

108. NEUMARK. L. M. 6 lines. (*Minor.*) G. NEUMARK, 1657.

109. SCHEFFLER. L. M. 6 lines. GERMAN.

112. SIBERIA. 8s & 7s. Unknown.

113. FOUNTAIN. 8s & 7s. M. D. Livensetter.

117. STUTTGARD. 8s & 7s. DRETZEL, 1731.

118. SCUDAMORE. 8s & 7s. R. R. CHOPE.

119. IAMBIC. 8s & 7s. Peculiar. J. Stobaeus, 1634.

120. REGENT SQUARE. 8s & 7s. Six lines. Dr. H. Smart.

121. SICILIAN HYMN. 8s & 7s. Six lines. Unknown.

122. DULCE CARMEN.   8s & 7s. Six lines.   Michael Haydn.

123. STOERL.   87, 87, 47.   J. G. C. Stoerl, 1744.

124. BENEDIC ANIMA.   8s & 7s. 6 lines.   Sir John Goss.

125. AUSTRIA.   8s & 7s. Double.   F. J. Haydn, 1797.

126. DEPARTURE. 8s & 7s. Double. M. D. LIVENSETTER.

127. MANT. 8s & 7s. Double. Scottish.

128. DARMSTADT. 8s & 7s. Double. Darmstadt Cant., 1688.

129. BAVARIA. 8s & 7s. Double. German.

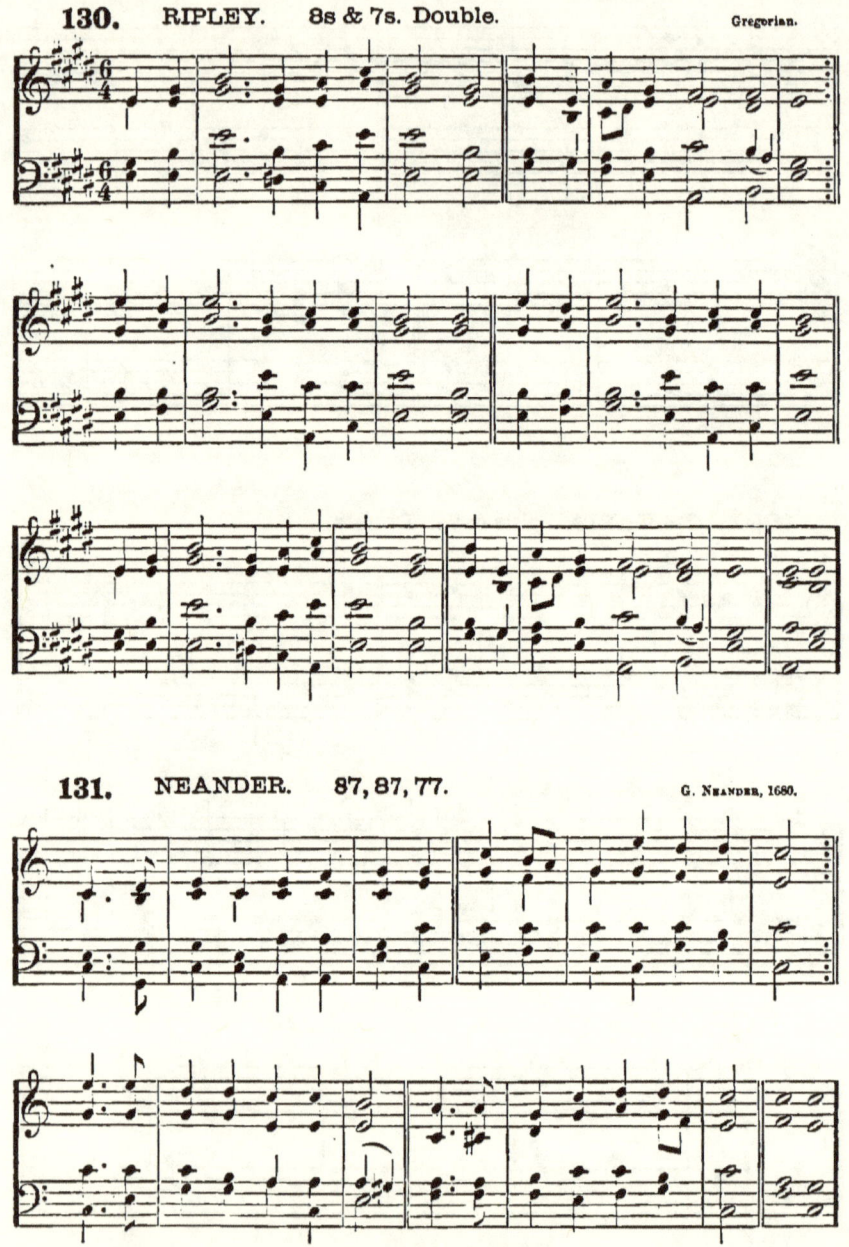

140. CALM. 86, 86, 88.   Thomas Hastings.

Ped.

147. WACHET AUF. 898, 898, 664, 88. P. Nicolai, 1599.

151. MONKLAND. 7s.
J. WILKES.

152. OLDENBERG 7s.
Old German.

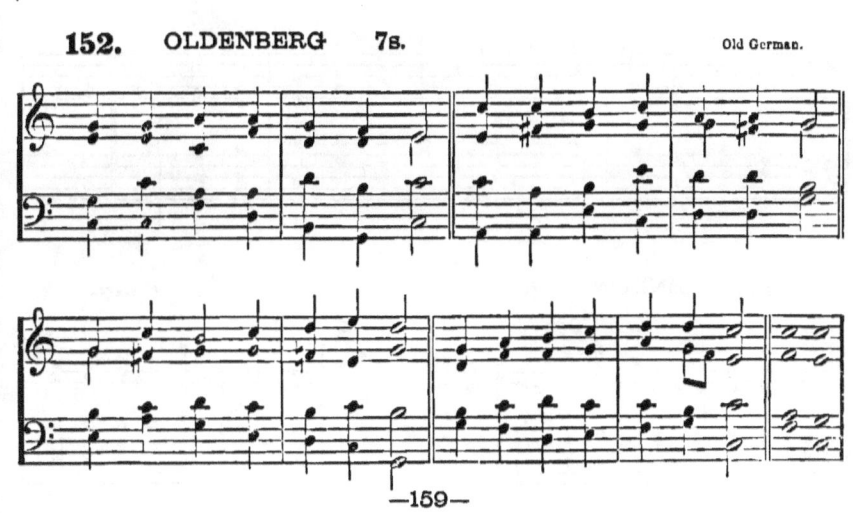

153. REDHEAD. 7s. R. REDHEAD.

154. VIENNA. 7s. G. H. KNECHT, 1793.

155. HENDON. 7s. CÆSAR MALAN.

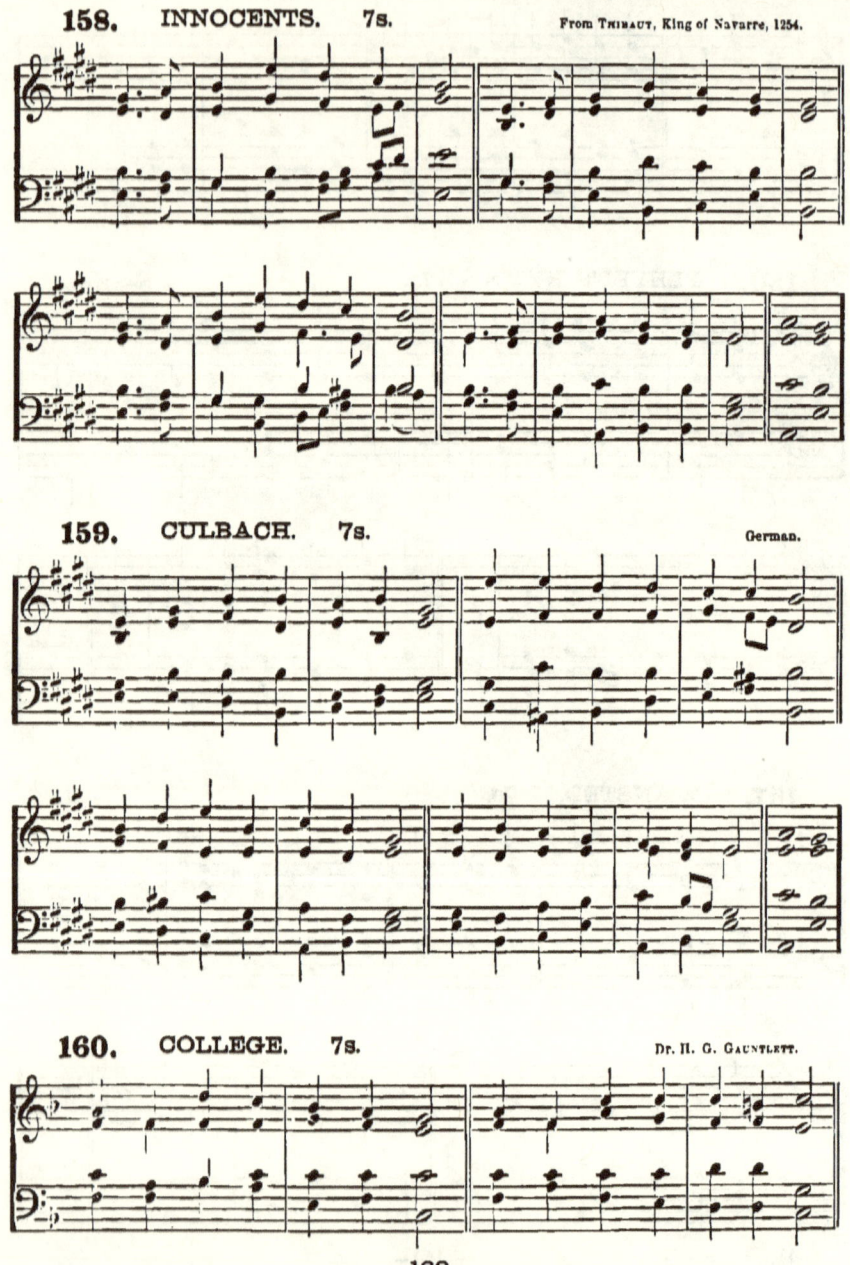

161. EDYFIELD. 7s.
C. G. Latrobe.

162. WEBER. 7s.
C. M. Von Weber.

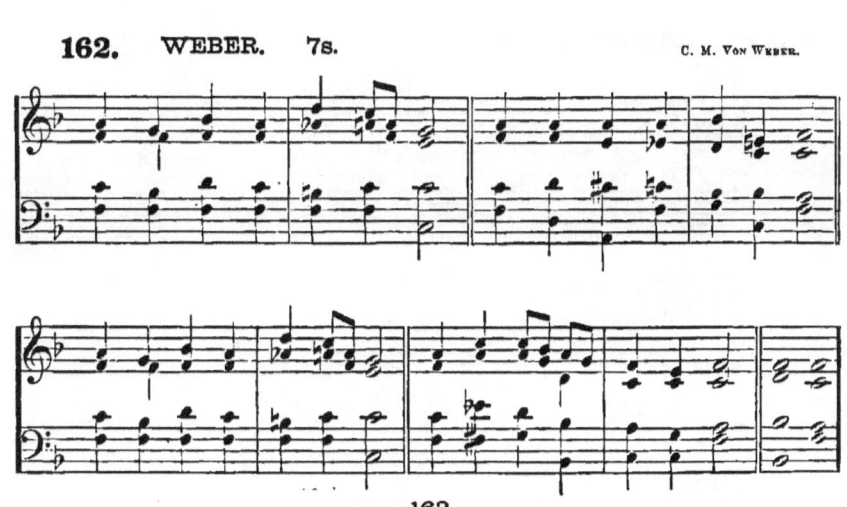

165. HORTON. 7s. C. Von Wartensee, 1780.

166. NUREMBURG. 7s. 6 lines. J. Rudolph Ahle, 1664.

169. DIX. 7s. 6 lines. CONRAD KOCHER.

170. HALLETT. 7s. 6 lines. J. H. Shepherd.

171. CALVARY. 7s. 6 lines. (*Minor.*) Jenks.

172. VENI SANCTE SPIRITUS. 7s. 6 lines, Peculiar.

Samuel Webbe.

173. MENDELSSOHN. 7s. Double. F. Mendelssohn.

174. ST. GEORGE. 7s. Double. Sir G. F. Elvey.

175. TICHFIELD. 7s. Double.   Unknown.

178. SPANISH HYMN. 7s. Double.

179. BOHEMIA. 7s & 6s. (*Trochaic.*) Bohemian, 1566.

183. ST. THEODULPH. 7s & 6s. Double. Melchior Teschner, 1613.

188. LAUSANNE.　　7s & 6s. Double.　　"Hamburg Psalter."

189. AURELIA. 7s & 6s. Double. S. S. Wesley.

190. EVARTS. 7s & 6s. Double.
German.

191. MISSIONARY HYMN. 7s & 6s. Double.
Dr. L. Mason, from the German.

192. DRETZEL. 78, 78, 77. U. Dretzel, 1731.

196. CALKIN. 76, 76, 88, 77. J. BAPTISTE CALKIN.

199. LAYRITZ. 6s. Peculiar. 4 or 6 lines. Dr. F. Layritz.

For Hymn 121 only.

Amen.

200. BETHANY. 64, 64, 664. Dr. L. Mason.

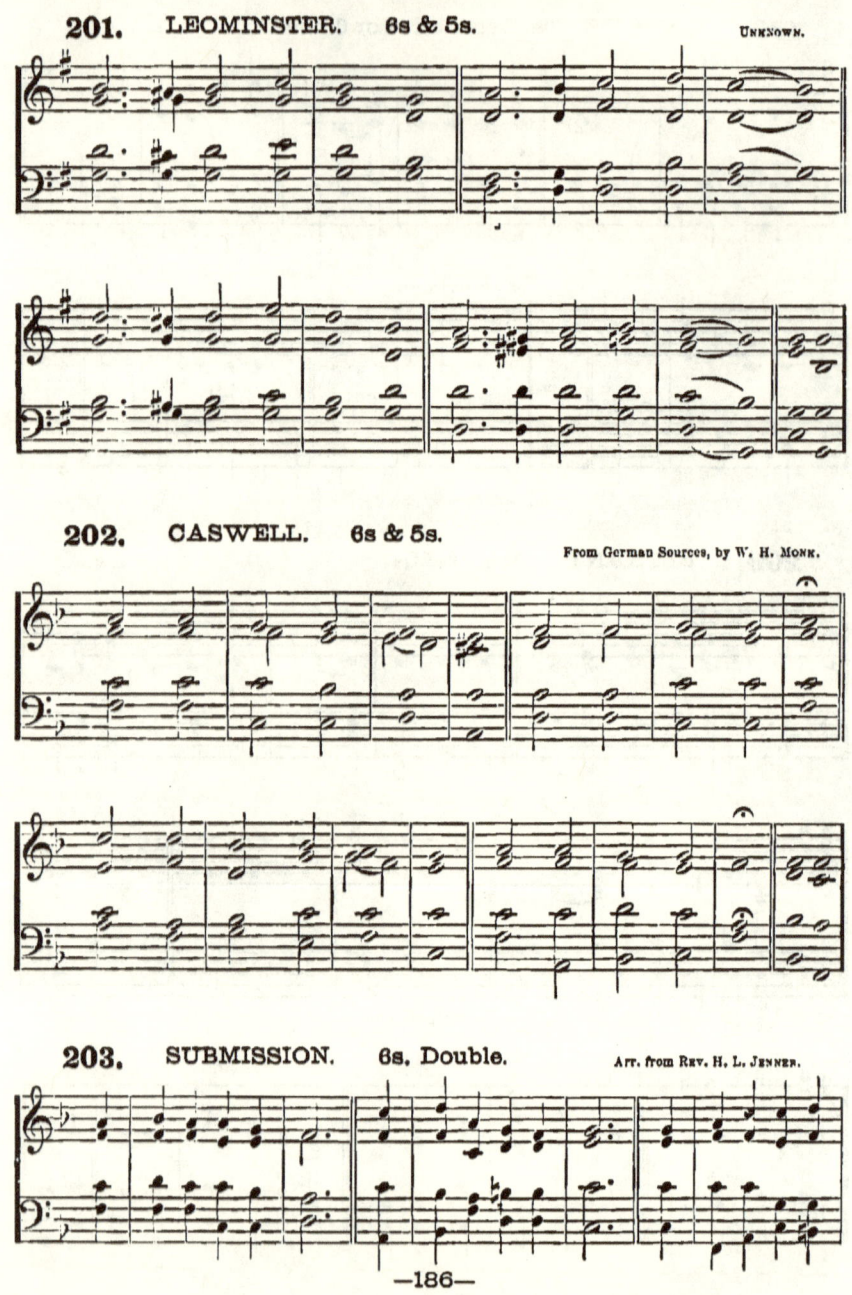

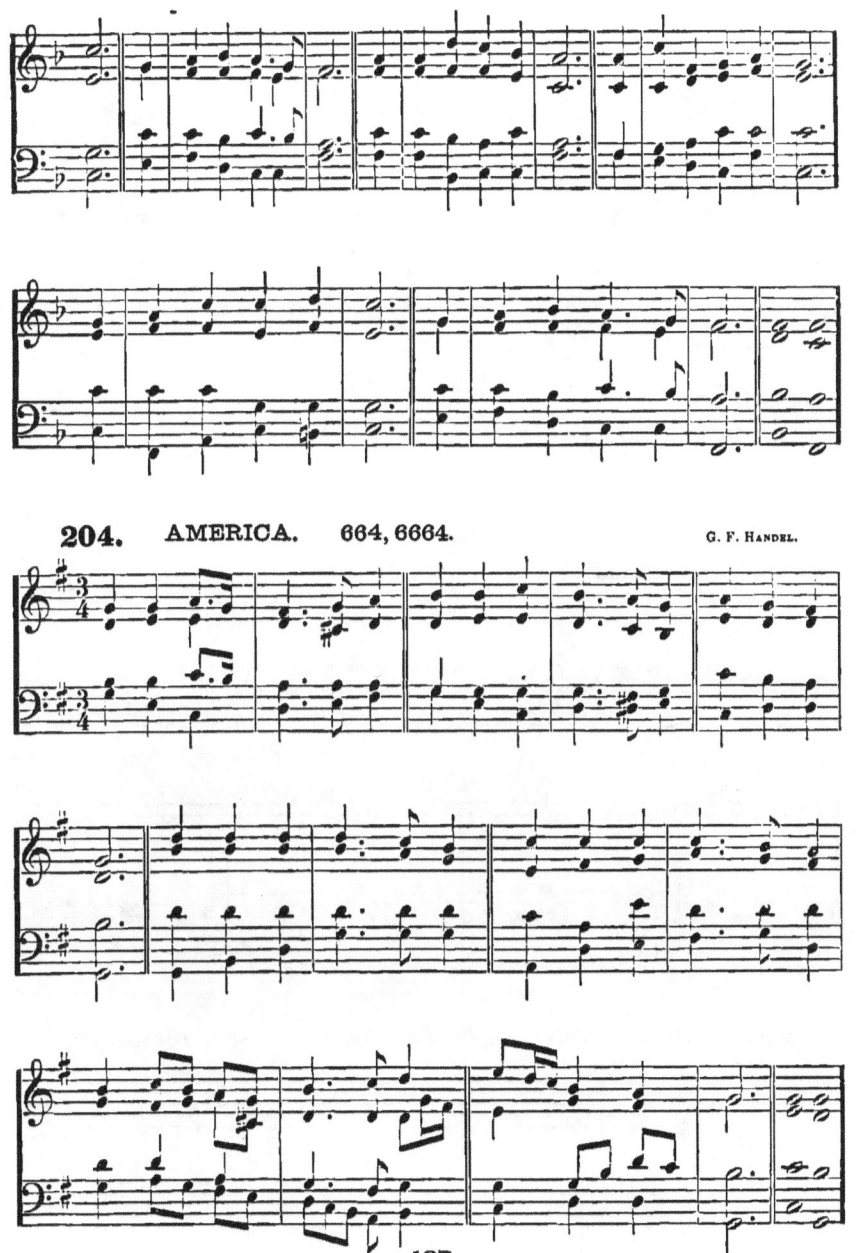

204. AMERICA. 664, 6664. G. F. HANDEL.

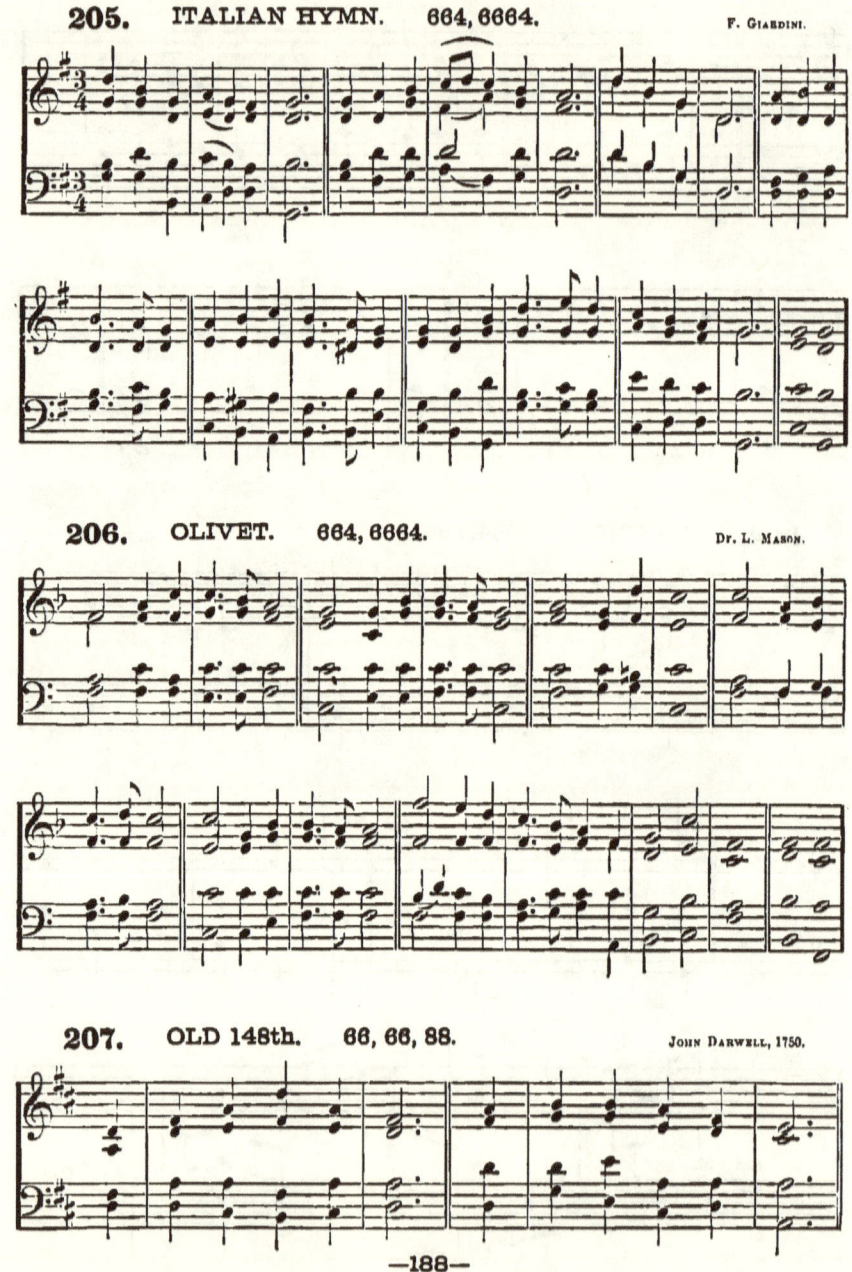

208. ST. GODRIC.   66, 66, 88.   Rev. J. B. Dykes.

211. LEONI. 66, 84. Double. *A Jewish Melody.*

214. ANGELICA. 10s.

E. J. Hopkins.

215. EVENTIDE. 10s. W. H. Monk.

216. PARADISE. 10, 6, 10, 6, 76, 76. Melchior Frank, 1608.

217. SEELENBRÄUTIGAM. 10s & 8s. 6 lines, Peculiar.
A. DRESE, 1698.

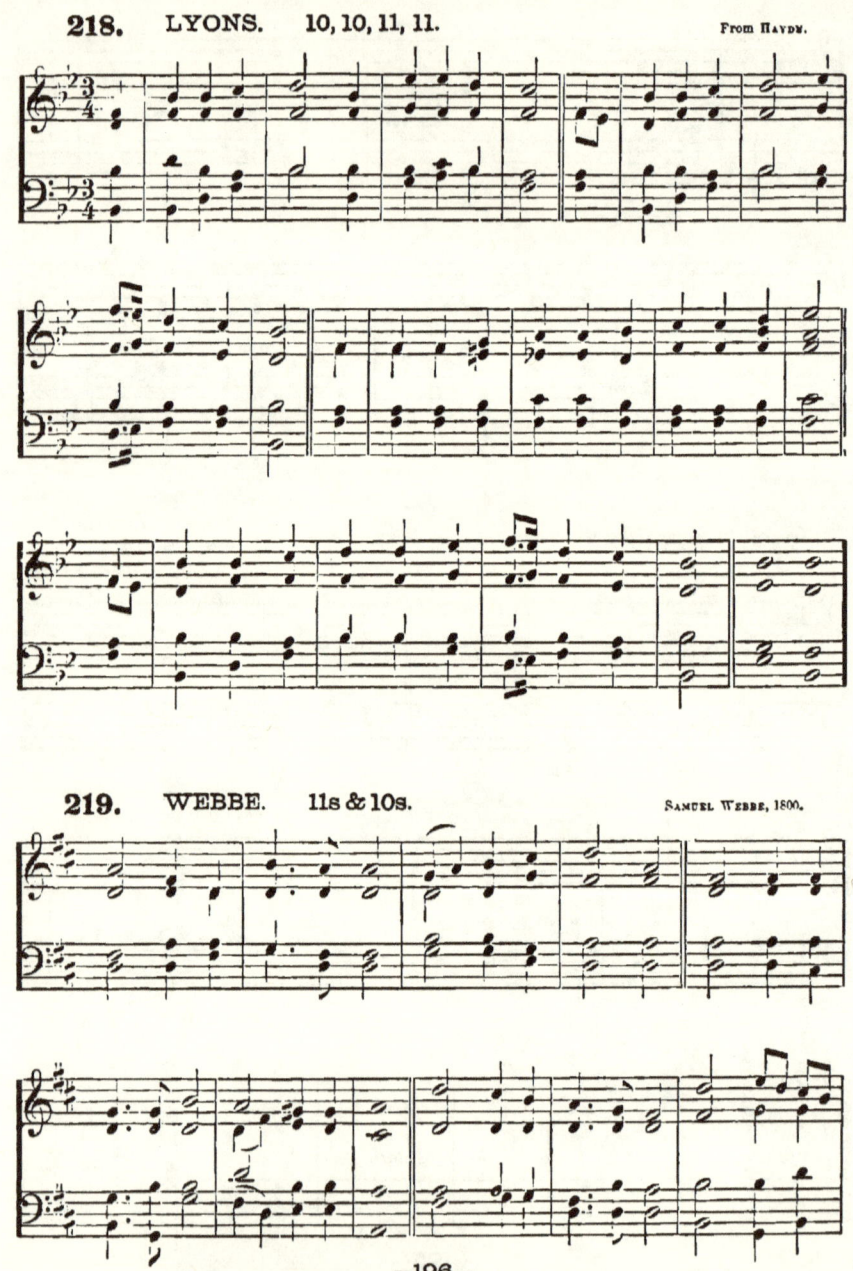

220. ADESTE FIDELES. 11s. JNO. READING, 1769.

223. OXFORD. 64, 64, 666, 4. HENRY SMART.

226. AINSWORTH. 86, 86, 88. 86. From "The Hallelujah."

229. ONWARD. 10s. Double. A. D. Merrill.

230. ROSSLYN. 11s & 8s. C. R. Cuff.

231. CORRIN. 11s & 8s. Peculiar. Unknown.

232. UNITY. 11, 11, 666, 5.   Unknown.

233. LOBE DEN HERREN. 14, 14, 11, 8.   From J. Neander, 1680.

234. SCOTLAND. **12s.** Dr. J. C. Whitefield.

The Repeat is for Chorus.

APPENDIX.

Additional Metrical Tunes.

235. HENRY. C. M. — S. B. Pond, 1835.

236. WOODSTOCK. C. M. — D. Dutton, Jr. 1829.

250. PARKER. C. M. WM. JACKSON.

251. ARLINGTON. C. M. THOS. A. ARNE, 1762.

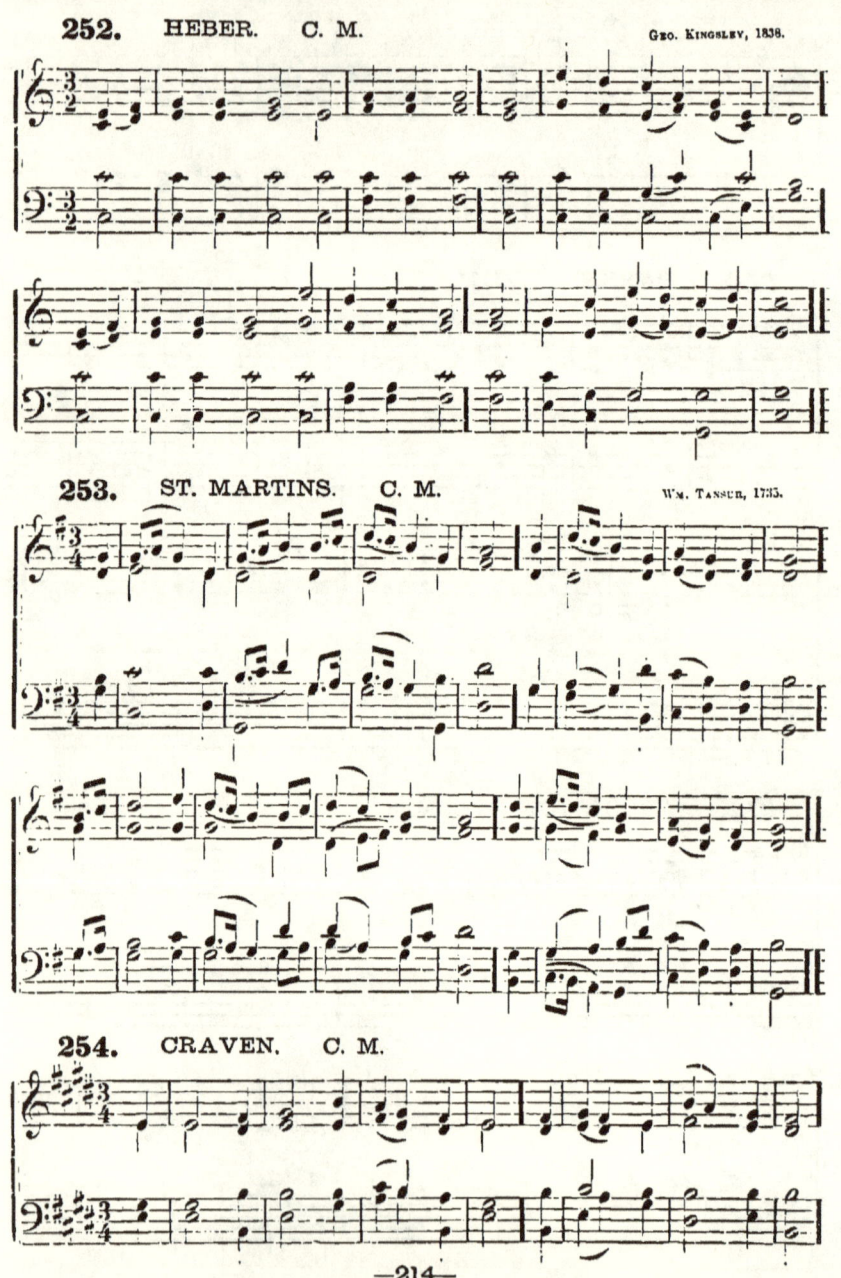

255. HEATH. C. M. L. Mason, 1835.

256. CLYDE. C. M. Double.

259. ATHENS. C. M. Double. F. GIARDINI.

263. LUTHER. S. M. — Thos. Hastings, 1855.

264. HOLBORN. S. M. — St. Alban's Tune Book.

265. ELMSWOOD. S. M. Double. *From the Dulcimer.*

266. LEBANON. S. M. Double. J. ZUNDEL.

267. ORLAND. L. M. Wm. Arnold, 1800.

268. ELPARAN. L. M. Schultz.

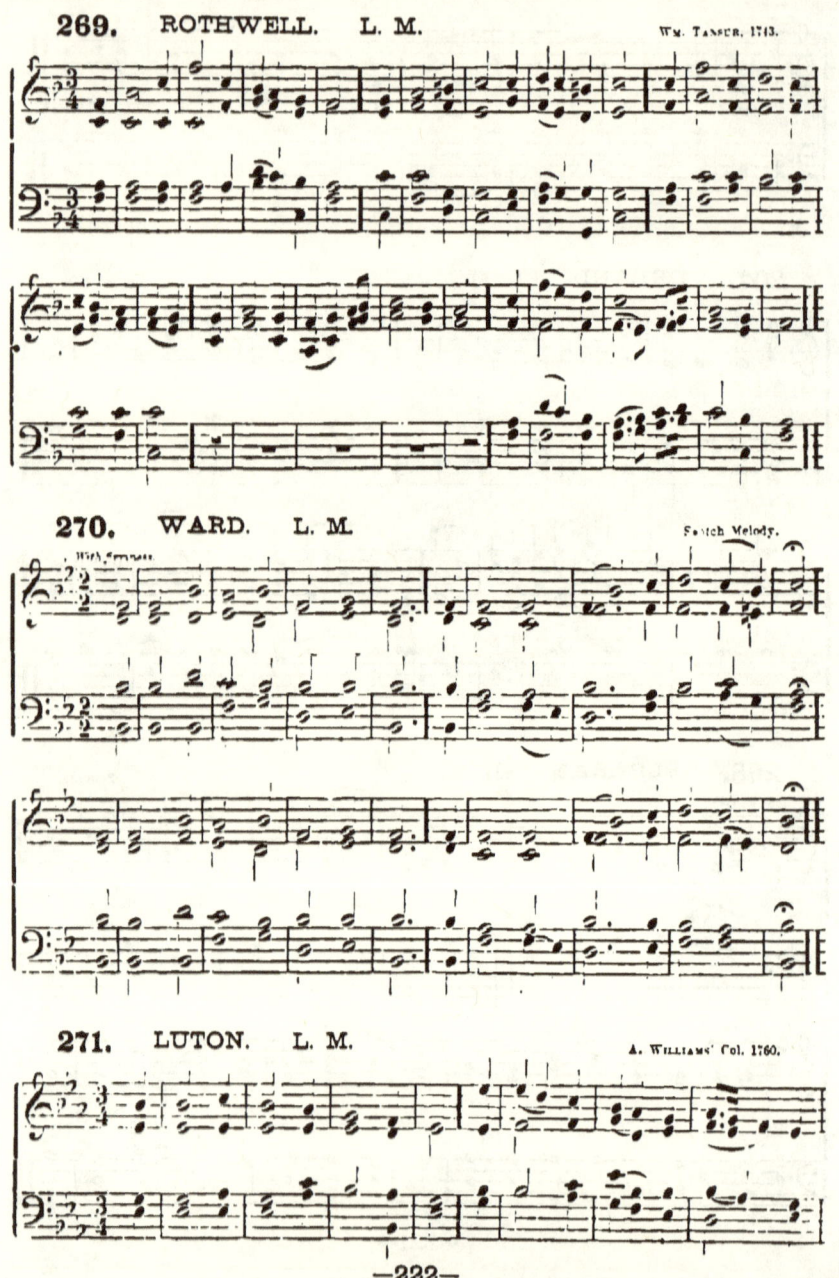

272. COMMUNION. L. M.

273. AMENIA. L. M. D, or 6 lines, omitting repeat. I. Baker.

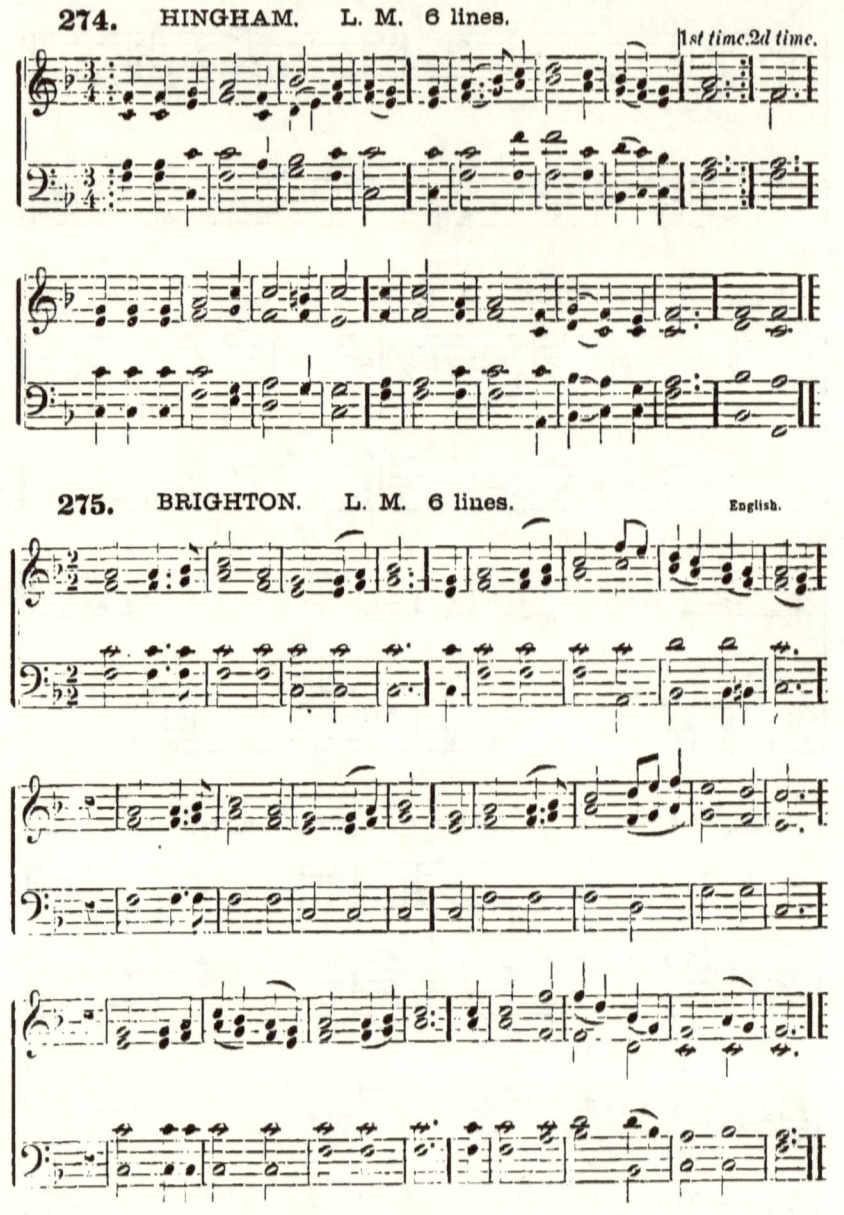

281. ZION. 8s, 7s, 4s. — Thos. Hastings, 1830.

282. HARWELL. 8, 7. Double. — L. Mason, 1840.

283. FLOTOW. 8, 7. Double. Arr. from Flotow.

284. GOODWIN. 7, 6. Double. G. J. Webb, 1837.

285. MENDEBRAS. 7, 6. Double. German Volkslied.

ALPHABETICAL INDEX.

Name of Tune.	Metre.	No.
Abridge	C. M.	38
Adeste Fideles	11s	220
Adolphus	886, 886	142
Ainsworth	86, 86, 88, 86	226
Aithlone	886, 886	144
Allemagne	87, 87, 77	132
Amenia	L. M. D.	273
America	664, 6664	204
Amsterdam	7s & 6s, D.,(*Peculiar*.)	198
Anatolius	76, 76, 88	195
Anfield	8s & 7s	114
Angelica	10s	214
Angel's Song	C. M. D.	46
Arlington	C. M.	251
Athens	C. M. D.	259
Aurelia	7s & 6s, D.	189
Austria	8s & 7s, D.	125
Bach	88, 77	149
Barby	C. M.	43
Barnby	C. M.	30
Bavaria	8s & 7s, D.	129
Bedford	C. M.	31
Belgrave	C. M.	32
Benedic Anima	8s & 7s, 6 lines	124
Benevento	7s, D.	279
Benevolence	L. M.	72
Bethany	64, 64, 664	200
Bethlehem	S. M.	52
Bishopthorpe	C. M.	9
Blendon	L. M.	79
Bohemia	7s & 6s, (*Trochaic*)	179
Bonn	L. M.	101
Bortmansky	7s, 6 lines	167
Brattle Street	C. M. D.	48
Brengle	L. M.	96
Brighton	L. M., 6 lines	275
Brown	C. M.	245
Brooklyn	H. M.	286
Burlington	C. M.	33
Calkin	76, 76, 88, 77	196
Calvary	7s 6 lines	171
Cambridge	S. M.	53
Calm	86, 86, 88	140
Carey	L. M., 6 lines	104
Caswell	6s & 5s	202
Chemnitz	L. M.	80
Chesterfield	C. M.	6

Name of Tune.	Metre.	No.
Chestnut Street	C. M.	241
Christmas	C. M.	37
Clarendon	C. M.	240
Clyde	C. M. D.	256
College	7s	160
Come	87, 87, 77	133
Communion	L. M.	272
Coronation	C. M.	4
Corrin	11s & 8s, (*Peculiar*)	231
Cowper	C. M.	243
Craven	C. M.	254
Creation	L. M., 6 lines	105
Crucifix	7s & 6s, D.	188
Cruger	C. M.	3
Culbach	7s	159
Darmstadt	8s & 7s, D.	128
Dedham	C. M.	246
Devotion	L. M., (*Peculiar*)	88
Dennis	S. M.	58
Departure	8s & 7s, D.	126
Diademata	S. M., D.	71
Dies Iræ	888	148
Dismission	L. M.	90
Dix	7s, 6 lines	169
Dorchester	C. M.	247
Dortmund	L. M.	100
Dover	S. M.	60
Dretzel	78, 78, 77	192
Duke Street	L. M.	81
Dulce Carmen	8s & 7s, 6 lines	122
Dundee	C. M.	248
Dwight	66, 86, 88	224
Eastburn	C. M.	242
Eaton	L. M., 6 lines	106
Eckardtsheim	C. M.	39
Edyfield	7s	161
Ein Feste Burg	L. M.	82
Ein Feste Burg Pr.	87, 87, 55, 56, 7	138
Elberfeld	87, 87, 887	139
Elmswood	S. M., D.	265
Elparan	L. M.	268
Ephrata	7s & 6s, D.	187
Eshtamoa	7s	276
Eternity	S. M.	63
Evarts	7s & 6s, D.	190
Eventide	10s	213
Ewing	7s & 6s, D.	185

ALPHABETICAL INDEX.

Name of Tune	Metre	No.	Name of Tune	Metre	No.
Fairfield	S. M., D	68	Leoni	66, 84, D	211
Federal Street	L. M	91	Lischer	H. M	288
Flotow	8s, 7s, D	283	Lobe den Herren	14, 14, 11, 8	233
Fountain	8s & 7s	113	Lob Gott	C. M	21
			Lowestoffe	C. M., D	45
Germany	L. M	98	Lubeck	78, 78, 77, (Peculiar)	193
Goodwin	7s & 6s, D	284	Luneberg	87, 87, 88	150
Gounod	87, 87, 77	135	Lurman	L. M	85
Greenfields	8s, D., (Peculiar)	228	Luther	S. M	263
Groton	555s & 11s, D	222	Luton	L. M	271
			Lyons	10, 10, 11, 11	218
Hague	C. M., D	258			
Hallett	7s, 6 lines	170	Manoah	C. M	8
Hamburg	L. M	92	Mant	8s & 7s, D	127
Harwell	8s & 7s, D	282	Martyn	7s, D	278
Hawley	C. M	17	Martyrdom	C. M	14
Heath	C. M	255	McEvers	S. M	260
Heber	C. M	252	Medfield	C. M	2
Helle Sonn	C. M	28	Meinhold	78, 78, 77	194
Hendon	7s	155	Mendebras	7s & 6s, D	285
Henry	C. M	235	Mendelssohn	7s, D	173
Herold	7s, D	176	Mendon	L. M	97
Hervey	C. M	40	Melita	L. M., 6 lines	103
Hingham	L. M., 6 lines	274	Meribah	886, 886	143
Hinton	11s	221	Migdol	L. M	87
Holborn	S. M	264	Miles Lane	C. M	25
Hollaz	8s & 7s	115	Missionary Hymn	7s & 6s, D	191
Holley	7s	163	Monk	S. M	51
Hollingside	7s, D	177	Monkland	7s	151
Horton	7s	165	Moredon	C. M	41
Hotham	7s, D	277	Morning Hymn	L. M	77
Hursley	L. M	93	Morning Star	887, 887, 88, 88	146
Iambic	8s & 7s, (Peculiar)	119	Naomi	C. M	238
Ilminster	C. M., D	47	Neander	87, 87, 77	131
Invitation	C. M	27	Neumark	L. M., 6 lines	108
Innocents	7s	158	Newcourt	L. M., P., 6 lines	110
Italian Hymn	664, 6664	205	Normanton	C. M	19
			Northampton	C. M	10
Jerusalem	C. M	22	Nun Danket	67, 67,66, 66	213
Judgment Hymn	87, 87, 887	137	Nuremburg	7s, 6 lines	166
			Nurnberg	L. M	75
Kane	S. M., D	70			
Konigsberg	87, 87, 77	134	O Ewigkeit	887, 887, 88	227
Knecht	C. M	12	Oldenburg	7s	152
			Old 100th	L. M	86
Laban	S. M	261	Old 148th	H. M	207
Lambert	L. M., 6 lines	107	Old 25th	S. M., D	67
Lancaster	C. M	15	Olivet	664, 6664	206
Lanesboro	C. M	1	Olney	S. M	57
Lausanne	7s & 6s, D	186	Onward	10s	229
Layritz	6s, P., (4 or 6 lines)	199	Orland	L. M	267
Lebanon	S. M., D	266	Ortonville	C. M	219
Leipsic	7s & 6s, (Trochaic)	181	Oxford	64, 64, 664	223
Lenox	H. M	287			
Lentz	L. M	73	Palestine	C. M	42
Leominster	Cs & 6s	201	Paradise	10, 6, 76, 76	216

ALPHABETICAL INDEX.

Name of Tune.	Metre.	No.
Parker	C. M	250
Park Street	L. M	76
Passion	S. M	61
Peldon	H. M	209
Penitence	L. M	94
Pleyel's Hymn	7s	156
Pollock	L. M	95
Potsdam	S. M	55
Rathbun	8s & 7s	111
Redhead	7s	153
Refuge	7s, 6 lines	168
Regent Square	8s & 7s, 6 lines	120
Resignation	86, 86, 88	141
Rest	6, 6, 11, D., (*Peculiar*)	212
Ripley	8s & 7s, D	130
Roe	8s & 7s	116
Romaine	7s & 6s, D	184
Rosslyn	11s & 8s	230
Rothwell	L. M	269
Rudolph	78, 78, 88	197
St. Agnes	C. M	7
St. Alphege	7s & 6s	180
St. Ann's	C. M	11
St. Etheldreda	C. M	20
St. Francis	C. M	36
St. George	7s, D	174
St. Godric	H. M	208
St. James	C. M	24
St. John's	C. M	237
St. Martin's	C. M	253
St. Michael	S. M	54
St. Peter	C. M	34
St. Stephens	C. M	13
St. Theodulph	7s & 6s, D	183
St. Thomas	S. M	50
Scheffler	L. M., 6 lines	109
Schneider	S. M	56
Scotland	12s	234
Scudamore	8s & 7s	118
Seelenbrautigam	10s & 8s, (*Peculiar*)	217
Shirland	S. M	262
Siberia	8s & 7s	112
Sicilian Hymn	8s & 7s, 6 lines	121
Sienna	S. M	62
Silver Street	S. M	49
Solitude	7s	164
Southwell	C. M	16

Name of Tune.	Metre.	No.
Spanish Hymn	7s, D	178
Steibelt	S. M	59
Stella	L. M	83
Stobaus	88, 88, 88, 66	145
Stockton	C. M	35
Stoerl	8s & 7s, 6 lines	123
Submission	6s, D	203
Stuttgard	8s & 7s	117
Swabia	S. M., D	66
Tallis' Ev'ing Hy.	L. M	78
Thatcher	S. M	64
Theoctistus	76, 88, 77	289
Thessalonica	S. M., D	69
Tichfield	7s, D	175
Tiverton	C. M	23
Toplady	7s, 6 lines	280
Trias	C. M	18
Triumph	76, 776	225
Truro	L. M	84
Unity	11, 11, 666, 5	232
Varina	C. M	257
Veni Sanctus Spir.	7s, 6 lines, (*Peculiar*)	172
Vespers	L. M	102
Vienna	7s	154
Vigils	C. M	5
Vulpius	7s & 6s	182
Wachet Auf	898, 898, 66, 4, 88, P.	147
Wansted	7s	157
Ward	L. M	270
Wareham	L. M	89
Warwick	C. M	239
Webbe	11s & 10s	219
Weber	7s	162
Weimar	S. M	65
Wer Gott Vertraut	8s & 7s, D., (*Pec.*)	136
Wells	L. M	99
Westlake	C. M., D	44
Wiltshire	C. M	29
Winchester	L. M	74
Windsor	C. M	26
Woodstock	C. M	236
Zanesville	C. M	244
Zebulon	H. M	210
Zion	8s & 7s	281

METRICAL INDEX.

Common Metre, 86, 86.

	No.
Abridge	38
Barby	43
Barnby	30
Bedford	31
Belgrave	32
Bishopthorpe	9
Burlington	33
Chesterfield	6
Christmas	37
Coronation	4
Crüger	3
Eckardtsheim	39
Hawley	17
Helle Sonn	28
Hervey	40
Invitation	27
Jerusalem	22
Knecht	12
Lancaster	15
Lanesboro	1
Lob Gott	21
Manoah	8
Martyrdom, (*Avon*)	14
Medfield	2
Miles Lane	25
Moredon	41
Normanton, (*Phuvah*)	19
Northampton	10
Palestine	42
St. Agnes	7
St. Ann's	11
St. Etheldreda	20
St. Francis	36
St. James	24
St. Peter	34
St. Stephens, (*Nayland*)	13
Southwell	16
Stockton	35
Tiverton	23
Trias	18
Vigils	5
Wiltshire	29
Windsor, (*Dundee*)	26

Com. Metre, Double.

	No.
Angels' Song	46
Brattle Street	48
Ilminster	47
Lowestoffe	45
Westlake	44

Short Metre, 66, 86.

	No.
Bethlehem	52
Cambridge	53
Dennis	58
Dover	60
Eternity	63
Monk	51
Olney	57
Passion	61
Potsdam	55
St. Michael	54
St. Thomas	50
Schneider	56
Sienna	62
Silver Street	49
Steibelt	59
Thatcher	64
Weimar	65

Short Metre, Double.

	No.
Diademata	71
Fairfield	68
Kane	70
Old 25th	67
Swabia	66
Thessalonica	69

Long Metre, 88, 88.

	No.
Benevolence	72
Blendon	79
Bonn	101
Brengle	96
Chemnitz	80
Devotion, (*Peculiar*)	88
Dismission	90
Dortmund	100
Duke Street	81
Ein Feste Burg	82
Federal Street	91
Germany	98
Hamburg	92
Hursley	93
Lentz	73
Lurman	85
Mendon	97
Migdol	87
Morning Hymn	77
Nüremburg	75
Old 100th	86

METRICAL INDEX.

	No.
Park Street	76
Penitence	94
Pollock	95
Stella	83
Tallis' Evening Hymn	78
Truro	84
Vespers	102
Wells	99
Wareham, (*All Saints*)	89
Winchester	74

Long Metre, 6 lines.

	No.
Carey	104
Creation	105
Eaton	106
Lambert	107
Melita	103
Neümark	108
Newcourt, (*Peculiar*)	110
Scheffler	109

8s & 7s, 87, 87.

	No.
Anfield	114
Fountain	113
Hollaz	115
Iambic, (*Peculiar*)	119
Rathbun	111
Roe	116
Scudamore	118
Siberia	112
Stuttgard	117

8s & 7s, 6 lines.

	No.
Benedic Anima	124
Dulce Carmen	122
Regent Square	120

	No.
Sicilian Hymn	121
Stoerl	123

8s & 7s, Double.

	No.
Austria	125
Bavaria	129
Darmstadt	128
Departure	126
Mant	127
Ripley	130
Wer Gott Vertraut (*Pec*)	136

87, 87, 77.

	No.
Allemagne	132
Come	133
Gounod	135
Königsberg	134
Neander	131

87, 87, 88, 7.

	No.
Elberfeld	139
Judgment Hymn	137

87, 87, 55, 56, 7.

	No.
Ein Feste Burg	138

86, 86, 88.

	No.
Calm	140
Resignation	141

886, 886.

	No.
Adolphus	142
Aithlone	144
Meribah	143

88, 88, 88, 66.

	No.
Stobäus	145

887, 887 88, 88.

	No.
Morning Star	146

898, 898, 66, 4, 88.

	No.
Wachet Auf	147

888.

	No.
Dies Ira	148

88, 77.

	No.
Bach	149

87, 87, 88.

	No.
Lüneberg	150

7s, 4 lines.

	No.
College	160
Culbach	159
Edyfield	161
Hendon	155
Holley	163
Horton	165
Innocents	158
Monkland	151
Oldenberg	152
Pleyel's Hymn	156
Redhead	153
Solitude	164
Vienna	154
Wansted	157
Weber	162

7s, 6 lines.

	No.
Bortmansky	167
Calvary	171
Dix	169
Hallett	170

METRICAL INDEX.

	No.
Nuremburg	166
Refuge	168
Veni Sanctus Spi., (*Pec.*)	172

7s. Double.

Herold	176
Hollingside	177
Mendelssohn	173
St. George	174
Spanish Hymn	178
Tichfield	175

7s & 6s.

Bohemia, (*Trochaic*)	179
Leipsic, (*Trochaic*)	181
St. Alphege	180
Vulpius	182

7s & 6s, Double.

Amsterdam, (*Peculiar*)	198
Aurelia	189
Crucifix	188
Ephrata	187
Evarts	190
Ewing	185
Lausanne	186
Missionary Hymn	191
Romaine	184
St. Theodulph	183

78, 78, 77.

Dretzel	192
Lubeck, (*Peculiar*)	193
Meinhold	194

76, 76, 88.

Anatolius	195

76, 76, 88, 77.

	No.
Calkin	196

78, 78, 88.

Rudolph	197

64, 64, 664.

Bethany	200

6s & 5s.

Caswall	202
Leominster	201

6s.

Layritz, (*Peculiar*)	199
Submission, (*Double*)	203

664, 6664.

America	204
Italian Hymn	205
Olivet	206

H. M. 66, 66, 88.

Old 148th	207
St. Godric	208
Zebulon	210

66, 66, 888.

Peldon	209

66, 84, Double.

Leoni	211

66, 11, Double.

Rest	212

67, 67, 66, 66.

Nun Danket	213

10s.

Angelica	214
Eventide	215
Onward	229

10, 67, 67, 6.

	No.
Paradise	216

10s & 8s, Peculiar.

Seelenbräutigam	217

10, 10, 11, 11.

Lyons	218

11s & 10s.

Webbe	219

11s.

Adeste Fideles	220
Hinton	221

555, 11, Double.

Groton	222

64, 64, 66, 64.

Oxford	223

66, 86, 88.

Dwight	224

76, 776.

Triumph	225

86, 86, 88, 86.

Ainsworth	226

887, 887, 88.

O Ewigkeit	227

8s, Double, Peculiar.

Greenfields	228

11s & 8s.

Corrin, (*Peculiar*)	231
Rosslyn	230

11, 11, 66, 65.

Unity	232

12s.

Scotland	234

14, 14, 11, 8.

Lobe den Herren	233

INDEX TO APPENDIX.

Name of Tune.	Metre.	No.
Amenia	L. M., Double	273
Arlington	C. M.	251
Athens	C. M., Double	259
Benevento	7s, Double	279
Brighton	L. M., 6 lines	275
Brooklyn	H. M.	286
Brown	C. M.	245
Chestnut Street	C. M.	241
Clarendon	C. M.	240
Clyde	C. M., Double	256
Communion	L. M.	272
Cowper	C. M.	243
Craven	C. M.	254
Dedham	C. M.	246
Dorchester	C. M.	247
Dundee	C. M.	248
Eastburn	C. M.	242
Elmswood	S. M., Double	265
Elparan	L. M.	268
Eshtamoa	7s	276
Flotow	7, 6, Double	283
Goodwin	7, 6, Double	284
Hague	C. M., Double	258
Harwell	8, 7, Double	282
Heath	C. M.	255
Heber	C. M.	252
Henry	C. M.	235
Hingham	L. M., 6 lines	274
Holborn	S. M.	264
Hotham	7s, Double	277

Name of Tune.	Metre.	No.
Laban	S. M.	261
Lebanon	S. M., Double	266
Lenox	H. M.	287
Lischer	H. M.	288
Luther	S. M.	263
Luton	L. M.	271
Martyn	7s, Double	278
McEvers	S. M.	260
Mendebras	7, 6, Double	285
Naomi	C. M.	238
O Paradise		24
Orland	L. M.	267
Ortonville	C. M.	249
Parker	C. M.	250
Rothwell	L. M.	269
St. John's	C. M.	237
St. Martin's	C. M.	253
Shirland	S. M.	262
Theoctistus	76, 88, 77	289
Toplady	7s, 6 lines	280
Varina	C. M., Double	257
Ward	L. M.	270
Warwick	C. M.	239
Woodstock	C. M.	236
Zanesville	C. M.	244
Zion	8, 7, 4, 7	281

CHORISTER'S REGISTER.
BOOK OF WORSHIP, (SOUTH.)

The Figures in the margin give the number of the Hymns in the Books in regular succession; opposite each of these is the name and number of the Tune or Tunes suited to it.

1. Ein Feste Burg, 82; Mendon, 97; Old 100th, 86.
2. St. Ann's, 11; Vigils, 5.
3. St. Stephens, 13; Helle Sonn, 28.
4. Mendon, 97; Brengle, 96.
5. Pleyel's Hymn, 156; Edyfield, 161.
6. Carey, 104; Scheffler, 109.
7. Helle Sonn, 28; Belgrave, 32.
8. Wells, 99; Federal St., 91.
9. Pleyel's Hymn, 156; Edyfield, 161.
10. Rosslyn, 230.
11. Hallett, 170; Bortmansky, 167; Herold, 176.
12. Silver St., 49; Olney, 57.
13. Mant, 127; Departure, 126.
14. Tichfield, 175; St. George, 174.
15. Park St., 76; Duke St., 81.
16. Lurman, 85; Wareham, 89.
17. Martyrdom, 14; St. James, 24; Lanesboro, 1.
18. Manoah, 8; St. Agnes, 7.
19. Ein Feste Burg, 82; Mendon, 97.
20. Adolphus, 142; Aithlone, 144.
21. St. Ann's, 11; Lancaster, 15.
22. Normanton, 19; Helle Sonn, 28.
23. Northampton, 10; Lanesboro, 1.
24. Wiltshire, 29; Stockton, 35.
25. Olney, 57; Cambridge, 53.
26. Schneider, 56; Eternity, 63.
27. Kane, 70; St. Thomas, 50.
28. Mendon, 97; Dortmund, 100.
29. Hinton, 221.
30. Carey, 104; Eaton, 106.
31. Martyrdom, 14; St. Ann's, 11.
32. Lyons, 218.
33. Ein Feste Burg, 82; Park St., 76.
34. Brattle St., 48; St. Agnes, 7.
35. Old 100th, 86; Mendon, 97.
36. Herold, 176; Horton, 165; Spanish Hymn, 178.
37. Eckardtsheim, 39; St. Agnes, 7.
38. St. Stephens, 13; St. Agnes, 7.
39. Wareham, 89; Dortmund, 100.
40. Lobe den Herren, 233.
41. Newcourt, 110.
42. Adolphus, 142; Meribah, 143.
43. Creation, 105, (*repeating first two strains*) Truro, 84.
44. Corrin, 231.
45. Old 100th, 86; Ein Feste Burg, 82.
46. Peldon, 209; Zebulon, 210.
47. Silver St., 49; Postdam, 55.
48. St. Stephens, 13; St. Etheldreda, 20.
49. Spanish Hymn, 178; Herold, 176.
50. Adeste Fideles, 220.
51. Rest, 212.
52. Roe, 116; Rathbun, 111.
53. Sicilian Hymn, 121; Regent Square, 120.
54. Southwell, 16; Hawley, 17; Medfield, 2.
55. Mendelssohn, 173; Hendon, 155.
56. Angelica, 214.
57. Bavaria, 129; Mant, 127.
58. Eckardtsheim, 39; St. Agnes, 7.
59. Christmas, 37; Angels' Song, 46.
60. Avison, (*Sunday-school Book, No. 82.*)
61. Carey, 104; Scheffler, 109.
62. Come, 133; Allemagne, 132.
63. Stoerl, 123; Dulce Carmen, 122.
64. Barby, 43; Abridge, 38.
65. Germany, 98; Blendon, 79.
66. St. Stephens, 13: St. Ann's, 11.
67. Invitation, 27; Vigils, 5.
68. Ein Feste Burg, (*proper;*) 138.
69. Adolphus, 142; (*omit notes between the stars.*)
70. Helle Sonn, 28; St. Agnes, 7.
71. Hamburg, 92; Wareham, 89.
72. Migdol, 87; Ein Feste Burg, 82.
73. Manoah, 8; Trias, 18.
74. Helle Sonn, 28; Wiltshire, 29.
75. Ewing, 185; Lausanne, 186.
76. Bonn, 101; Migdol, 87.
77. Adolphus, 142; Meribah, 143.
78. Dennis, 58; Thatcher, 64.
79. Adolphus, 142; Aithlone, 144.
80. St. Peter, 34; St. Etheldreda, 20.
81. Lanesboro, 1; Cruger, 3.
82. Dennis, 58; Dover, 60.
83. Herold, 176; Spanish Hymn, 178.
84. Pollock, 95; Vespers, 102.
85. Crucifix, 188; Missionary Hymn, 191.
86. Germany, 98; Federal St., 91.
87. Neander, 131; Gounod, 135.
88. Hursley, 93; Federal St., 91.
89. Roe, 116; Hollaz, 115; Bavaria, 129.

CHORISTER'S REGISTER.—BOOK OF WORSHIP, SOUTH.)

90. Culbach, 139; Innocents, 158.
91. Mendelssohn, 173; St. George, 174; Hendon, 155.
92. Cambridge, 53; Olney, 57.
93. Calm, 140.
94. Innocents, 158; Hendon, 155.
95. Zebulon, 210; Old 144th, 207.
96. Hendon, 155; Innocents, 158.
97. Mendon, 97; Brengle, 96.
98. Coronation, 4; Miles Lane, 25.
99. Christmas, 37; Chesterfield, 6; Hawley, 17.
100. Christmas, 37; Tiverton, 23.
101. Bonn, 101; Tallis' Evening Hymn, 78.
102. Stockton, 35; Burlington, 33; Lanesboro, 1.
103. Hinton, 221.
104. Rathbun, 111; Siberia, 112.
105. Allemagne, 192; Neander, 131.
106. Hervey, 49; Tiverton, 23.
107. Wells, 99; Bonn, 101.
108. Barby, 43; Martyrdom, 14.
109. Dover, 60; Weimar, 65.
110. St. Agnes, 7; Barby, 43.
111. Wareham, 59; Penitence, 94.
112. Mant, 127; Darmstadt, 128.
113. Lurman, 85; Federal St., 91.
114. St. Ann's, 11; Tiverton, 23.
115. St. Stephens, 13; Northampton, 10.
116. St. Thomas, 50; Monk, 51.
117. Federal St., 91; Hamburg, 92.
118. Blendon, 79; Duke St., 81.
119. Sicilian Hymn, 121; Regent Square, 120.
120. Lurman, 85; Wareham, 59.
121. Sicilian Hymn, 121; Stoerl, 123.
122. Angelica, 214.
123. Sicilian Hymn, 121; Regent Square, 120.
124. Potsdam, 55; Olney, 57.
125. Lob Gott, 21; Jerusalem, 22.
126. Mendelssohn, 173; St. George, 174.
127. Mendon, 97; Chemnitz, 80.
128. Ripley, 130; Darmstadt, 128.
129. Ein Feste Burg, 82; Migdol, 87.
130. Olney, 57; Dennis, 58.
131. Pleyel's Hymn, 156; Edyfield, 161.
132. Northampton, 10; Invitation, 27.
133. Old 134th, 86; Brengle, 96.
134. Chesterfield, 6; Barby, 43.
135. Old 144th, 207; Zebulon, 210.
136. Steibelt, 59; Weimar, 65; Silver St., 49.
137. Manoah, 8; Bedford, 31.
138. Blendon, 79; Duke St., 81.
139. Abridge, 38; St. Francis, 36.
140. Christmas, 37; Burlington, 33.
141. Mant, 127; Bavaria, 129.
142. Dortmund, 100; Brengle, 96.
143. Rathbun, 111; Siberia, 112.
144. Medfield, 2; Northampton, 10.
145. Hinton, 221.
146. St. Agnes, 7; Manoah, 8.
147. Thatcher, 64; St. Thomas, 50.
148. Weimar, 65; Thatcher, 64.
149. Migdol, 87; Ein Feste Burg, 82.
150. Federal St., 91; Pollock, 95.
151. Bishopthorpe, 9; Northampton, 10.
152. Tallis' Evening Hymn, 78; Penitence, 94.
153. Old 25th, 67; Fairfield, 68.
154. Vigils, 5; Bishopthorpe, 9.
155. Invitation, 27; Lob Gott, 21.
156. Roe, 116; Siberia, 112.
157. Old 100th, 86; Pollock, 95.
158. Manoah, 8; Martyrdom, 14.
159. Mant, 127; Roe, 116.
160. Old 100th, 86; Pollock, 95.
161. Martyrdom, 14; Vigils, 5.
162. St. Ann's, 11; Bedford, 31.
163. St. Agnes, 7; Manoah, 8; St. Ann's, 11.
164. Vigils, 5; Manoah, 8.
165. Stella, 83; Tallis' Evening Hymn, 78.
166. Migdol, 87; Creation, 105; Dortmund, 100.
167. Lurman, 85; Brengle, 96.
168. Vigils, 5; Burlington, 33.
169. Blendon, 79; Lurman, 85; Stella, 83.
170. St. Agnes, 7; Trias, 18.
171. Germany, 93; Migdol, 87.
172. Bonn, 101; Federal St., 91.
173. Manoah, 8; St. Stephens, 13.
174. Migdol, 87; Wareham, 59.
175. Olney, 57; St. Thomas, 50.
176. Martyrdom, 14; Trias, 18.
177. Horton, 165; Wansted, 157.
178. Duke St., 81; Hursley, 93.
179. Wiltshire, 29; Tiverton, 23.
180. Invitation, 27; Martyrdom, 14.
181. Dover, 60; Steibelt, 59.
182. Silver St., 49; Dover, 60.
183. Helle Sonn, 28; Eckardsheim, 89.
184. Morning Hymn, 77; Chemnitz, 80.
185. Hursley, 93; Nurnberg, 75.
186. Martyrdom, 14; Wiltshire, 29.
187. Thatcher, 64; Cambridge, 53.
188. Belgrave, 32; Trias, 18.
189. Redhead, 173; Solitude, 164.
190. St Alphege, 180; Vulpius, 192.
191. Tallis' Evening Hymn, 78; Mendon, 97.
192. Penitence, 94; Hursley, 93.
193. Tallis' Evening Hymn, 78; Dismission, 90.
194. Barby, 43; Abridge, 38.
195. Devotion, 88; Greenfields, 225.
196. Edyfield, 161; Innocents, 158.

—240—

CHORISTER'S REGISTER.—BOOK OF WORSHIP, (SOUTH.)

197. Weber, 162; Edyfield, 161.
198. Bavaria, 129; Ripley, 130.
199. Duke St., 81; Stella, 83.
200. St. Francis, 36; Palestine, 42.
201. Palestine, 42; St. Francis, 36; St. Etheldreda, 20.
202. Moredon, 41; Manoah, 8.
203. Winchester, 74; Nurnberg, 75.
204. Mendon, 97; Wells, 99.
205. Wiltshire, 29; St. Agnes, 7.
206. Migdol, 87; Creation, 105; Federal St., 91.
207. Austria, 125; Departure, 126; Darmstadt, 128.
208. Dover, 60; Olney, 57.
209. Innocents, 158; Pleyel's Hymn, 156.
210. Meribah, 143; Aithlone, 144.
211. Vespers, 102; Tallis' Evening Hymn, 78.
212. Belgrave, 32; Abridge, 38.
213. Ripley, 130; Austria, 125.
214. Vespers, 102; Brengle, 96.
215. Vigils, 5; St. Agnes, 7.
216. Trias, 18; Palestine, 42.
217. Duke St., 81; Migdol, 87.
218. St. Ann's, 11; St. Stephens, 13.
219. St. Agnes, 7; Manoah, 8.
220. Belgrave, 32; Trias, 18.
221. Amsterdam, 198.
222. Vigils, 5, Manoah, 8; Brattle St., 48.
223. Winchester, 74; Benevolence, 72.
224. Martyrdom, 14; St. Agnes, 7.
225. St. Agnes, 7; Chesterfield, 6.
226. Winchester, 74; Truro, 84.
227. Olney, 57; Dover, 60.
228. Manoah, 8; Eckardtsheim, 39.
229. Benevolence, 72; Winchester, 74.
230. Solitude, 164; Holley, 163; Pleyel's Hymn, 156.
231. Benevolence, 72; Migdol, 87.
232. Hursley, 93; Migdol, 87; Benevolence, 72.
233. Kane, 70; St. Thomas, 50.
234. Northampton, 10; Tiverton, 23.
235. Mant, 127; Darmstadt, 128; Bavaria, 129.
236. Brattle St., 48; Lancaster, 15.
237. Lancaster, 15; Lanesboro, 1.
238. Fairfield, 68; Diademata, 71; Olney, 57.
239. Jerusalem, 22; Wiltshire, 29.
240. Martyrdom, 14; Northampton, 10.
241. St. Thomas, 50, Bethlehem, 52.
242. Stoerl, 123; Benedic Anima, 124.
243. Lanesboro, 1; Helle Sonn, 28.
244. Winchester, 74; Ein Feste Burg, 82.
245. St. Stephens, 13; Abridge, 38.
246. Lanesboro, 1; Helle Sonn, 28; Manoah, 8.
247. Resignation, 141; Calm, 140.

248. Invitation, 27; Jerusalem, 22.
249. St. Agnes, 7; Helle Sonn, 28.
250. Ripley, 130; Bavaria, 129.
251. Normanton, 19; Tiverton, 23.
252. St. Agnes, 7; Lanesboro, 1.
253. Trias, 18; Lanesboro, 1.
254. Wareham, 89 Germauy, 98.
255. Wareham, 89; Brengle, 96.
256. Barby, 43; St. Stephens, 13.
257. Barby, 43; Eckardtsheim, 39.
258. Lentz, 73; Migdol, 87.
259. Carey, 104; Eaton, 106.
260. Webbe, 219.
261. Winchester, 74 Brengle, 96.
262. Sicilian Hymn, 121; Stoerl, 123.
263. Wareham, 89; Dismission, 90.
264. Olney, 57; Dover, 60.
265. Invitation, 27; Barby, 43.
266. St. Agnes, 7; Trias, 18.
267. Wiltshire, 29; Helle Sonn, 28.
268. Weber, 162; Edyfield, 161.
269. Scotland, 234.
270. Spanish Hymn, 178.
271. Bortmansky, 167; Refuge, 168.
272 Oxford, 223.
273. Ainsworth, 226.
274. Hinton, 221.
275. Edyfield, 161.
276. Rosslyn, 230; (*omitting ties.*)
277. Edyfield, 161; Weber, 162.
278. Sicilian Hymn, 121; Stoerl, 123.
279. Weber, 162; Pleyel's Hymn, 156.
280. Barby, 43; Manoah, 8.
281. Chemnitz, 80; Duke St., 81.
282. Innocents, 158; College, 160.
283. Culbach, 159; Innocents, 158.
284. Herold, 176; Spanish Hymn, 178.
285. Amsterdam, 198.
286. Wareham, 89; Vespers, 102.
287. Dortmund, 100; Chemnitz, 80.
288. Calvary, 171; Refuge, 168.
289. Edyfield, 161; Weber, 162.
290. Warcham, 89; Brengle, 96.
291. Moredon, 41; St. Francis, 36.
292. Diademata, 71; Fairfield, 68.
293. Olney, 57; Dover, 60.
294. Roe, 116; Fountain, 113.
295. O Ewigkeit, 227.
296. Wareham, 89; Dismission, 90.
297. Meribah, 143.
298. Blendon, 79; Federal St., 91; (*repeating last two syllables.*)
299. Penitence, 94; Pollock, 95.
300. Federal, St., 91; Hursley, 93.

CHORISTER'S REGISTER.—BOOK OF WORSHIP, (SOUTH.)

301. Meribah, 143; Althlone, 144.
302. Penitence, 94; Dortmund, 100.
303. Come, 133; Konigsberg, 134.
304. Penitence, 94; Nurnberg, 75.
305. Edyfield, 161; Herold, 176;
     Pleyel's Hymn, 156.
306. Wells, 99; Federal St., 91.
307. Vigils, 5; St. Agnes, 7.
308. St. Thomas, 50; Schneider, 56.
309. Chesterfield, 6; Bishopthorpe, 9.
310. Dix, 169; Bortnansky, 167.
311. Rosslyn, 230; (omitting the ties.)
312. Ein Feste Burg, 82; (repeating first half,)
     Carey, 104.
313. Pleyel's Hymn, 156; Weber, 162.
314. Peldon, 209; Old 148th, 207.
315. Northampton, 10; Barby, 43.
316. Weimar, 65; Olney, 57.
317. St. Etheldreda, 20; Trias, 18.
318. Mant, 127; Darmstadt, 128; Bavaria, 129.
319. Manoah, 8; Martyrdom, 14.
320. Migdol, 87; Duke St., 81.
321. Eventide, 215.
322. Vigils, 5; Tiverton, 23.
323. Manoah, 8; Northampton, 10.
324. Regent Square, 120; Stoerl, 123.
325. Winchester, 74; Stella, 83.
326. Manoah, 8; Bishopthorpe, 9.
327. St. Theodulph, 183; Ewing, 185.
328. Wiltshire, 29; Invitation, 27.
329. Helle Sonn, 28; Burlington, 33.
330. Rathbun, 111; Fountain, 113.
331. Scotland, 234.
332. Fountain, 113; add "Far at Sea" to beginning
     of last line of each verse.
333. Tiverton, 23; Lob Gott, 21.
334. Innocents, 158; Monkland, 151.
335. Federal St., 91; Penitence, 94.
336. Federal St., 91; Penitence, 94.
337. Ein Feste Burg, 82; Chemnitz, 80.
338. Manoah, 8; Martyrdom, 14.
339. Chemnitz, 80; Blendon, 79.
340. Hamburg, 92; Wareham, 89.
341. Christmas, 37; Miles Lane, 25.
342. Abridge, 38; Normanton, 19.
343. St. Thomas, 50; Weimar, 65.
344. Chemnitz, 80; Morning Hymn, 77.
345. Weimar, 65; Silver St., 49.
346. Weimar, 65; Steibelt, 59.
347. Refuge, 168; Hallett, 170; Calvary, 171.
348. Hollingside, 177; Herold, 176,
     Spanish Hymn, 178.
349. Abridge, 38; Barby, 43; Lanesboro, 1.
350. Manoah, 8; Trias, 18.

351. Nurnberg, 75; Wareham, 89.
352. Bethany, 200; Oxford, 223; (omitting ties.)
353. Hursley, 93; Penitence, 94.
354. Thatcher, 64; Passion, 61.
355. Duke St., 81; Lurman, 85.
356. Manoah, 8; Palestine, 42.
357. Manoah, 8; St. Stephens, 13.
358. St. Agnes, 7; Manoah, 8.
359. Hamburg, 92; Dortmund, 100.
360. Eternity, 63; Dennis, 58.
361. Migdol, 87; Park St., 76.
362. Hursley, 93; Old 100th, 86.
363. Brengle, 96; Dortmund, 100.
364. St. Ann's, 11; Martyrdom, 14.
365. Allemagne, 132; Neander, 131.
366. Dix, 169.
367. Winchester, 74; Pollock, 95.
368. Migdol, 87; Federal St., 91
369. Tallis' Evening Hymn, 78; Stella, 83.
370. Adolphus, 142; Meribah, 143.
371. Jerusalem, 22; St. Francis, 36.
372. Penitence, 94; Germany, 98.
373. Hinton, 221 (omitting chorus.)
374. Onward, 229; Angelica, 214.
375. Crucifix, 188; Evarts, 190.
376. St Thomas, 50; St. Michael, 54.
377. Dennis, 58; Dover, 60.
378. Lanesboro, 1; Northampton, 19.
379. St. Michael, 54; Thatcher, 64.
380. St. Agnes, 7; Chesterfield, 6.
381. St. Godric, 208; Zebulon, 210.
382. Mendon, 97; Duke St., 81.
383. Bonn, 103. Federal St., 91.
384. Hollingside, 177; Spanish Hymn, 178.
385. Ein Feste Burg, 82; Mendon, 97.
386. Zebulon, 210; Peldon, 209.
387. Tiverton, 23; Lanesboro, 1.
388. Barby, 43; Abridge, 38.
389. Missionary Hymn, 191; St. Theodulph, 183.
390. Benedic Anima, 124; Stoerl, 123.
391. Wells, 99; Migdol, 87.
392. Eventide, 215.
393. Austria, 125, (omit repeat.)
394. Missionary Hymn, 191; Ephrata, 187.
395. Lanesboro, 1; Chesterfield, 6.
396. Chemnitz, 80; Duke St., 81.
397. St. Agnes, 7; Martyrdom, 14.
398. Stella, 83; Hamburg, 92.
399. Lentz, 73; Nurnberg, 75.
400. St. Agnes, 7; Helle Sonn, 28.
401. Christmas, 37; Eckartsheim, 39.
402. Eckartsheim, 39; Burlington, 33.
403. Moredon, 41; Barby, 43.
404. Abridge, 38; Bedford, 81.

CHORISTER'S REGISTER.—BOOK OF WORSHIP, (SOUTH.)

405. Hursley, 93; Federal St., 91.
406. Manoah, 8; Abridge, 38.
407. Manoah, 8; Moredon, 41.
408. Nuruberg, 75; Mendon, 97.
410. Old 100th, 86; Chemnitz, 80.
411. Old 100th, 86; Federal St., 91.
412. Monkland, 151; Hendon, 155.
413. Meribah, 143.
414. St. Agnes, 7; Abridge, 38.
415. Calm, 140; Resignation, 141.
416. Hervey, 40; Stockton, 35.
417. Amsterdam, 198.
418. Old 100th, 86; Hamburg, 92.
419. Resignation, 141.
420. Meribah, 143; (*slurring 2d and 3d, 4th and 5th notes of third and last strains.*)
421. Old 100th, 86; Tallis' Evening Hymn, 78.
422. Wells, 99; Bonn, 101.
423. Adolphus, 142; Aithlone, 144.
424. Vigils, 5; Martyrdom, 14.
425. Martyrdom, 14; Vigils, 5.
426. Dwight, 224.
427. Stella, 83; Wareham, 89; Federal, St., 91.
428. Windsor, 26.
429. Hamburg, 92; (*repeating last line.*)
430. Meribah, 143; Aithlone, 144.
431. Penitence, 94; Hamburg, 92.
432. Stella, 83; Pollock, 95.
433. Pollock, 95; Wareham, 89.
434. Silver St., 49; Dover, 60.
435. Eventide, 215.
436. Hinton, 221.
437. Siberia, 112.
438. Submission, 203.
439. Scotland, 234.
440. Dennis, 58; Thatcher, 64.
441. Old 100th, 86; Hamburg, 92.
442. Sienna, 62; Dover, 60.
443. Barby, 43; Northampton, 10.
444. Lanesboro, 1; Manoah, 8.
445. Eckardtsheim, 39; Abridge, 38.
446. Stoerl, 123; Regent Sq., 120; Sicilian Hy., 121.
447. Dover, 60; Weimar, 65.
448. Regent Square, 120; Stoerl, 123.
449. Judgment Hymn, 137; Elberfeld, 139.
450. Old 100th, 86.
451. Edyfield. 161; (*add first line to end of each verse.*)
452. Jerusalem, 22; St. Agnes, 7; Wiltshire, 29.
453. Herold, 176; Hollingside, 177.
454. Manoah, 8; Belgrave, 32.
455. Lanesboro, 1.
456. Manoah, 8; St. Agnes, 7.
458. Invitation, 27; Wiltshire, 29.
459. Sicilian Hymn, 121.
460. Unity, 232.
461. Refuge, 168.
462. Ein Feste Burg, 82; Old 100th, 86.
463. Thatcher, 64; Olney, 57.
464. Mendon, 97; Brengle, 96.
465. Roe, 116; Anfield, 114; Fountain, 113.

CHORISTER'S REGISTER.

BOOK OF WORSHIP, (NORTH.)

The Figures in the margin give the number of the Hymns in the Books in regular succession; opposite each of these is the name and number of the Tune or Tunes suited to it.

1. Ein Feste Burg, 82; Mendon, 97; Old 100th, 86.
2. Schneider, 56; Eternity, 63.
3. Olney, 57; Cambridge, 53.
4. Rosslyn, 230.
5. Lyons, 218.
6. Silver St., 49; Potsdam, 55; Steibelt, 59.
7. Olney. 57; Silver St., 49.
8. Zebulon, 210; Old 148th, 207.
9. Wells, 99; Ein Feste Burg, 82.
10. Hinton, 221.
11. Rathbun, 111; Siberia, 112.
12. Olney. 57; Silver St., 49.
13. Wells, 99; Duke St., 81.
14. Hervey. 40; Tiverton, 23.
15. Peldon, 209; Zebulon, 210.
16. Rathbun. 111; Scudamore, 118; Fountain, 113.
17. Newcourt, 110.
18. Northampton, 10; Lanesboro, 1.
19. Cambridge, 53; St. Thomas, 50.
20. Edyfield, 161; Pleyel's Hymn, 156.
21. Nuremburg, 166; Dix, 169.
22. Mendon, 97; Wells, 99.
23. Duke St., 81; Hursley, 93.
24. Wareham, 89; Federal St., 91.
25. St. Agnes, 7; Manoah, 8.
26. Pleyel's Hymn, 156; Edyfield, 161.
27. Regent Square, 120; Sicilian Hymn, 121.
28. St. Stephens, 13; St. Agnes, 7; Abridge, 38.
29. Mendon, 97; Winchester, 74.
30. St. Stephens. 13; Lanesboro, 1.
31. Sicilian Hymn, 121; Stoerl, 123.
32. Olney, 57; St. Thomas, 50.
33. Duke St., 81; Truro, 84.
34. Silver St., 49; Olney, 57.
35. Zebulon, 210; Peldon, 209.
36. Hallett, 170; Bortmansky, 167; Herold, 176.
37. Zebulon, 210; Peldon, 209.
38. Hursley, 93; Nurnberg, 75.
39. St. Agnes, 7; Manoah, 8; St. Ann's, 11.
40. St. Thomas, 50; Thatcher, 64.
41. Missionary Hymn, 191; St. Theodulph, 183.
42. Wells. 99; Federal St., 91.
43. Migdol, 87; Creation, 105; Dortmund, 100.
44. Olney, 57; Potsdam, 55.
45. Belgrave, 32; Tiverton, 23.
46. Mendon, 97; Brengle, 96.
47. Helle Sonn, 28; Belgrave, 32.
48. Old 148th, 207; Zebulon, 210.
49. Migdol, 87; Mendon, 97.
51. Brattle St., 48; Lancaster, 15.
52. Duke St., 81; Stella, 83.
53. Monkland, 151; Innocents, 158.
54. Manoah, 8; St. Agnes, 7.
55. Martyrdom, 14; St. James, 24; Lanesboro, 1.
56. Wareham, 89; Chemnitz, 80.
57. Normanton, 19; Helle Sonn, 23.
58. Pollock, 95; Penitence, 94.
59. Ein Feste Burg, 82; Truro, 84.
60. Lanesboro. 1; Abridge, 38.
61. Meribah, 143; Adolphus, 142.
62. Rathbun, 111; Fountain, 113.
63. Bonn. 101; Penitence, 94.
64. Olney, 57; Potsdam, 55; Dover, 60.
65. Christmas, 37; Helle Sonn, 28.
66. Italian Hymn, 203; America, 204.
67. Hendon, 155; College, 160.
68. Creation, 105; *(repeating first two strains.)* Truro, 84.
69. Medfield, 2; St. Ann's, 11.
70. Wareham, 89; Lurman, 85.
71. Lob Gott, 21; Abridge, 38.
72. Wiltshire 29; Tiverton, 23.
73. Carey, 104; Eaton, 106.
74. Dover, 60; Potsdam, 55.
75. Northampton, 10; Tiverton, 23.
76. St. Stephens, 13; St. Agnes, 7.
77. Eckardtsheim. 39; St. Agnes, 7.
78. Mendon, 97; Bonn. 101.
79. Moredon, 41; *(repeating second half.)*
80. Ein Feste Burg, 82; Park St., 76.
81. Tiverton, 23; Lob Gott, 21.
82. Kane, 70; Olney, 57.
83. St. Stephens, 13; Southwell, 16.
84. Peldon, 209; Zebulon, 210.
85. Chemnitz, 80; Morning Hymn, 77.
86. Trias, 18; Belgrave, 32.
87. Burlington, 33; Lanesboro, 1.
88. Trias. 18; Palestine, 42.
89. Old 100th, 86; Dortmund, 100.
90. Hamburg, 92; Vespers, 102.

CHORISTER'S REGISTER.—BOOK OF WORSHIP, (NORTH.)

91. Barby, 43.
92. Dismission, 90; Penitence, 94.
93. Eckardtsheim, 39; Hervey, 40.
94. Steibelt, 59; Weimar, 65; Silver St., 49.
95. Weimar, 65; Silver St., 49.
96. Benedic Anima, 124; Sicilian Hymn, 121.
97. Rosslyn, 230.
98. Brengle, 96; Mendon, 97.
99. Thessalonica, 69.
100. St. Etheldreda, 20; Belgrave, 22.
101. St. Ann's, 11; Lancaster, 15.
102. Christmas, 37; Burlington, 33.
103. Duke St., 81; Ein Feste Burg, 82.
104. Christmas, 37; Wiltshire, 29.
105. Lob Gott, 21; Normanton, 19.
106. Helle Sonn, 28; Wiltshire, 29.
107. Burlington, 33; Barby, 43.
108. Anfield, 114; Hollaz, 115.
109. St. Stephens, 13; Wiltshire, 29.
110. Christmas, 37; Chesterfield, 6; Hawley, 17.
111. Southwell, 16; Hawley, 17; Medfield, 2.
112. Coronation, 4; Cruger, 3.
113. Old 148th, 207; Zebulon, 210.
114. St. Thomas, 50; Potsdam, 55.
115. Hamburg, 92; Federal St., 91.
116. Hamburg, 92; Nurnberg, 75.
117. Helle Sonn, 28; St. Agnes, 7.
118. Martyrdom, 14; Invitation, 27.
119. Blendon, 79; Stella, 83.
120. Refuge, 168; Calvary, 171.
121. Barnby, 30; Stockton, 35.
122. Ilminster, 47; Lowestoffe, 45.
123. Old 100th, 86; Wells, 99.
124. Hervey 40; Abridge, 38.
125. Pollock, 95; Vespers, 102.
126. Hinton, 221.
127. Winchester, 74; Nurnberg, 75.
128. Trias, 18; Palestine, 42.
129. Palestine, 42; Barby, 43.
130. Crucifix, 188; Missionary Hymn, 191.
131. Schneider, 56; Passion, 61.
132. Roe, 116; Hollaz. 115; Bavaria, 129.
133. Scudamore, 118; Siberia, 112.
134. St. Stephens, 13; St. Ann's, 11.
135. Dennis, 58; Thatcher, 64.
136. Abridge, 38; St. Francis, 36.
137. Pollock, 95; Nurnberg, 75.
138. Stoerl, 123; Dulce Carmen, 122.
139. St. Etheldreda, 20; Wiltshire, 29.
140. Germany, 98; Federal St., 91.
142. Peldon, 209; Old 148th, 207.
143. Migdol, 87; Ein Feste Burg, 82.
144. Zebulon, 210; St. Godric, 208.
145. Peldon, 209; Zebulon, 210.
146. Blendon, 79; *(repeat last two syllables.)*
147. Blendon, 79; Dismission, 90.
148. Scheffler, 109; Eaton, 106.
149. Coronation, 4; Miles Lane, 25.
150. Bavaria, 129; Mant, 127.
151. Stockton, 35; Burlington, 33.
152. Helle Sonn, 28; Abridge, 38.
153. St. Theodulph, 183; Romaine, 184.
154. Austria, 125; Bavaria, 129.
155. Chesterfield, 6; Barby, 43.
156. Manoah, 8; Medfield, 2.
157. Normanton, 19; Vigils, 5.
158. Hendon, 155; Monkland, 151.
159. Adolphus, 142; Meribah, 143.
160. Christmas, 37; Tiverton, 23.
161. Migdol, 87; Park St., 76.
162. Allemagne, 132; Neander, 131.
163. Zebulon, 210; Old 148th, 207.
164. Park St., 76; Migdol, 87.
165. Lanesboro, 1; Medfield, 2.
166. St. Agnes, 7; Chesterfield, 6.
167. Wareham, 89; Dortmund, 100.
168. Wansted, 157; Culbach, 159.
169. Migdol, 87; Park St., 76.
170. Angelica, 214.
171. Bonn, 101; Migdol, 87.
172. Mant, 127; Departure, 126.
173. Hallett, 170; Bortmansky, 167.
174. Chemnitz, 80; Blendon, 79.
175. St. Peter, 34; St. Etheldreda, 20.
176. Lob Gott, 21; Trias, 18.
177. Hervey, 40; Knecht, 12.
178. Adolphus. 142; Aithlone, 144.
179. Resignation, 111; Calm, 140.
180. Wells, 99; Bonn, 101,
181. Wareham, 89; Penitence, 94.
182. St. Agnes, 7; Barby, 43.
183. Germany, 98; Vespers, 102.
184. Scheffler, 109; Carey, 104.
185. Bonn, 101; Germany, 98.
186. Wansted, 157; Spanish Hymn, 178.
187. Oldenberg, 152; Pleyel's Hy., 156; Herold, 176.
188. Hursley, 93; Bonn, 101.
189. Northampton, 10; Bishopthorpe, 9.
190. Lurman, 85; Federal St., 91.
191. Cambridge, 53; Olney, 57.
192. Invitation, 27; Lanesboro, 1.
193. Ripley, 130; Darmstadt, 128.
194. Lanesboro, 1; Chesterfield, 6.
195. Mendon, 97; Truro, 84.
196. Italian Hymn, 205; America, 204.
197. Bishopthorpe, 9; Northampton, 10.
198. Thatcher, 64; St. Thomas, 50.
199. Adolphus, 142; Meribah, 143.

CHORISTER'S REGISTER.—BOOK OF WORSHIP, (NORTH.)

200. Migdol, 87; Ein Feste Burg, 82.
201. Missionary Hymn, 191.
202. Potsdam, 55; Olney, 57.
203. St. Stephens, 13; Wiltshire, 29.
204. Helle Sonn, 28; Bedford, 31.
205. St. Thomas, 50.
206. Sicilian Hymn, 121; Regent Square, 120.
207. Bedford, 31; Hervey, 40.
208. Sicilian Hymn, 121; Regent Square, 120.
209. Lurman, 85; Wareham, 89.
210. Chemnitz, 80; Wareham, 89.
211. Federal St., 91; Dortmund, 100.
212. Pleyel's Hymn, 156; Edyfield, 161.
213. Meudon, 97; Chemnitz, 80.
214. Monkland, 151; Wansted, 157.
215. Mendelssohn, 173; St. George, 174.
216. Barby, 43; Abridge, 38.
217. Spanish Hymn, 178; Herold, 176.
218. Weimar, 63; Silver St., 49.
219. Tiverton, 23; Lanesboro, 1.
220. Monkland, 151; Culbach, 159.
221. Missionary Hymn, 191; St. Theodulph, 183.
222. Kane, 70; Swabia, 66.
223. St. Alphege, 180; Vulpius, 82; Missionary Hymn, 191.
224. Ein Feste Burg, 82; Migdol, 87.
225. Park St., 76; Truro, 84.
226. Hinton, 221.
227. Lob Gott, 21; Burlington, 33.
228. Angelica, 214.
229. Roe, 116; Rathbun, 111.
230. Mendelssohn, 173; Hendon, 155.
231. Old 148th, 207; Zebulon, 210.
232. Eckardtsheim, 39; St. Agnes, 7.
233. Adeste Fideles, 220.
234. Sicilian Hymn, 121; Regent Square, 120.
235. Palestine, 12; Trias, 18.
236. Penitence, 94; Devotion, 88.
237. Herold, 176; Spanish Hymn, 178.
238. Vigils, 5; Martyrdom, 14.
239. Mendelssohn, 173; St. George, 174; Hendon, 155.
240. Old 148th, 207; Zebulon, 210.
241. Calm, 140.
242. Peldou, 209; Zebulon, 210.
243. Mendelssohn, 173; Monkland, 151; Hendon, 155.
244. Hendon, 155.
245. Ein Feste Burg, 82; Mendon, 97.
246. St. Ann's, 11; Tiverton, 23.
247. Blendon, 79; Migdol, 87.
248. Thatcher, 64; St. Thomas, 50.
249. Lanesboro, 1; Helle Sonn, 28; Manoah, 8.
250. Newcourt, 110.

251. Bishopthorpe, 9; St. Stephens, 13.
252. Normanton, 19; Tiverton, 23.
253. Bishopthorpe, 9; Northampton, 10.
254. Bonn, 101; Warebam, 89.
255. St. James, 24; Tiverton, 23.
256. Helle Sonn, 28; Vigils, 5.
257. Edyfield, 161; Holley, 163.
258. Roe, 116; Siberia, 112; Mant, 137.
259. Dortmund, 100; Hamburg, 92.
260. Hursley, 93; Pollock, 95.
261. Martyrdom, 14; Vigils, 5.
262. Old 100th, 86; Pollock, 95.
263. Old 100th, 86; Pollock, 95.
264. Northampton, 10; St. Ann's, 11.
265. Amsterdam, 198.
266. Calm, 140; Resignation, 141.
267. Hursley, 93; Park St., 76.
268. Crucifix, 188; Aurelia, 189; **Missionary Hymn**, 191.
269. Sicilian Hymn, 121.
270. Martyrdom, 14; Moredon, 41.
271. Olney, 57; Dover, 60.
272. Lanesboro, 1; Wiltshire, 29.
273. Come, 133; Konigsberg, 134.
274. Sicilian Hymn, 121.
275. Olney, 57; Thatcher, 64.
276. Solitude, 164; Edyfield, 161.
277. Wareham, 89; Vespers, 102.
278. Sicilian Hymn, 121; Stoerl, 123.
279. Weber, 162; Edyfield, 161.
280. Vespers, 102; Dortmund, 100.
281. Scotland, 234.
282. Old 148th, 207; Zebulon, 210.
283. Germany, 98; Blendon, 79.
284. Wareham, 89; Dismission, 90.
285. Dismission, 90; Wareham, 89.
286. Invitation, 27; Barby, 43.
287. Hervey, 40; Stockton, 35.
288. Chemnitz, 80; Duke St., 81.
289. Edyfield, 161; Weber, 162.
290. Hinton, 221.
291. Abridge, 38; Bedford, 31.
292. Dortmund, 100; Chemnitz, 80.
293. Vigils, 5; Barby, 43.
294. Dennis, 58; Steibelt, 39.
295. Moredon, 41; St. Francis, 136.
296. Adolphus, 142; Aithlone, 144.
297. Wells, 99; Bonn, 101.
298. Penitence, 94; Nurnberg, 75.
299. Moredon, 41; Manoah, 8.
300. Edyfield, 161; Herold, 176; **Pleyel's Hymn**, 156.
301. Penitence, 94; Pollock, 95.
302. Penitence, 94; Bonn, 101.

CHORISTER'S REGISTER.—BOOK OF WORSHIP, (NORTH.)

303. Amsterdam, 198.
304. Kane, 70; Fairfield, 68.
305. Adolphus, 112; Aithlone, 144.
306. Wareham, 89; Brengle, 96.
307. Hollaz, 115; Roe, 116; Fountain, 113.
308. Steibelt, 59; St. Thomas, 50.
309. Brengle, 96; Germany, 98.
310. Refuge, 168; Hallett, 170; Calvary, 171.
311. Blendon, 79; Federal St., 91; (*repeat last two syllables.*)
312. Meribah, 143; Aithlone, 144.
313. Crucifix, 188; Lausanne, 186.
314. Amsterdam, 198.
315. Invitation, 27; Burlington, 33.
316. Wells, 99; Federal St., 91.
317. Hallett, 170; Refuge, 168; Calvary, 171.
318. Trias, 18; Hervey, 40.
319. St. Ann's, 11; Abridge, 38.
320. Angels' Song, 46; Lowestoffe, 45.
321. Mendon, 97; Ein Feste Burg, 82.
322. Manoah, 8; Lob Gott, 21.
323. St. Agnes, 7; Manoah, 8.
324. Dover, 60; Weimar, 65.
325. Germany, 98; Migdol, 87.
326. St. Agnes, 7; Trias, 18.
327. Migdol, 87; Wareham, 89.
328. Stella, 83; Lurman, 85.
329. Webbe, 219.
330. Helle Sonn, 28; St. Agnes, 7.
331. Olney, 57; St. Thomas, 50.
332. Hervey, 40; Burlington, 33.
333. St. Agnes, 7; Chesterfield, 6.
334. Kane, 70; St. Thomas, 50; Olney, 57.
335. Jerusalem, 22; Wiltshire, 29.
336. Bortnansky, 167; Dix, 169.
337. Weber, 132; Edyfield, 161.
338. Stella, 83; Lurman, 85.
339. Invitation, 27; Tiverton, 23.
340. Migdol, 87; Federal St., 91.
341. Federal St., 91; Hamburg, 92.
342. Lowestoffe, 45; Brattle St., 48.
343. Jerusalem, 22; St. Francis, 36.
344. St. Agnes, 7; Hervey, 40; Eckardtsheim, 39.
345. St. Stephens, 13; Hervey, 40.
346. Submission, 203.
347. Submission, 203.
348. Barby, 43; Vigils, 5.
349. Hursley, 93; Pollock, 95.
350. Ripley, 130; Austria, 125.
351. Nuruberg, 75; Wareham, 89.
352. Penitence, 94; Dortmund, 100.
353. Fairfield, 68; Diademata, 71.
354. Belgrave, 39; Abridge, 38.
355. Dover, 60; Silver St., 49.
356. Thatcher, 64; Dennis, 58.
357. Belgrave, 32; Trias, 18.
358. Hollingside, 177; Herold, 176; Spanish Hymn, 178.
359. St. Ann's, 11; St. Stephens, 13.
360. Dortmund, 100; Bonn, 101.
361. Ein Feste Burg, 82; Mendon, 97.
362. Mant, 127; Ripley, 130.
363. Hinton, 221.
364. Olivet, 206; Italian Hymn, 205.
365. Dennis, 58; St. Michael, 54.
366. Lurman, 85; Wareham, 89.
367. St. Etheldreda, 20; Trias, 18.
368. St. Theodulph, 183; Missionary Hymn, 191.
369. Martyrdom, 14; Bishopthorpe, 9.
370. St. Agnes, 7; Chesterfield, 6.
371. Ein Feste Burg, 82; Chemnitz, 80.
372. Stella, 83; Dismission, 90.
373. Hinton, 221.
374. Lowestoffe, 45; Angels' Song, 46.
375. Hervey, 40; Vigils, 5.
376. Mendon, 97; Dortmund, 100.
377. Fairfield, 68; Thessalonica, 69.
378. St. Francis, 36; Palestine, 42.
379. Manoah, 8; St. Agnes, 7.
380. Aurelia, 189; Lausanne, 186.
381. Sienna, 62; Eternity, 63.
382. Crucifix, 188; St. Theodulph, 183.
383. Vigils, 5; Manoah, 8.
384. Barby, 43; Moredon, 41.
385. Mant, 127; Bavaria, 129.
386. Wareham, 89; Federal St., 91.
387. Stoerl, 123; Benedic Anima, 124.
388. Old 148th, 207; Zebulon, 210.
389. St. Ann's, 11; Belgrave, 32.
390. Wiltshire, 29; Helle Sonn, 28.
391. Steibelt, 59; Bethlehem, 52.
392. Abridge, 38; Barby, 43; Lanesboro, 1.
393. Bethany, 200; Oxford, 223; (*omitting ties.*)
394. Mant, 127; Roe, 116.
395. Palestine, 42; St. Francis, 36; St. Etheldreda, 20.
396. Siberia, 112; Anfield, 114.
397. Greenfields, 228.
398. Belgrave, 32; Vigils, 5.
399. Federal St., 91; Hamburg, 92.
400. Greenfields, 228.
401. Scheffler, 109; Melita, 103.
402. Hursley, 93; Penitence, 94.
403. Vespers, 102; Brengle, 96.
404. Manoah, 8; Invitation, 27.
405. St. Ann's, 11; Lob Gott, 21.
406. Barby, 43; St. Ann's, 11; Lob Gott, 21.
407. Amsterdam, 198.

CHORISTER'S REGISTER.—BOOK OF WORSHIP, (NORTH.)

408. Abridge, 38; Normanton, 19.
409. Federal St., 91; Brengle, 96.
410. Mendon, 97; Wells, 99.
411. Brengle, 96; Hamburg, 92.
412. Northampton, 10; Invitation, 27.
413. Federal St., 91; Chemnitz, 80.
414. Vigils, 5; St. Agnes, 7.
415. Amsterdam, 198.
416. Lurman, 85; Wareham, 89.
417. Federal St., 91; Truro, 84.
418. Weber, 162; Pleyel's Hymn, 156.
419. Manoah, 8; Palestine, 42.
420. Manoah, 8; Palestine, 42.
421. Thatcher, 64; Dover, 60.
422. Brengle, 96; Mendon, 97.
423. St. Ann's, 11; St. Stephens, 13.
424. Austria, 125; Departure, 126; Darmstadt, 128.
425. Tallis' Evening Hymn, 78; Stella, 83.
426. St. Etheldreda, 20; Tiverton, 23.
427. Hursley, 93; Migdol, 87; Benevolence, 72.
428. Dover, 60; Olney, 57.
429. Wiltshire, 29; St. Agnes, 7.
430. St. Agnes, 7; Chesterfield, 6.
431. Federal St., 91; Brengle, 96.
432. St. Michael, 54; St. Thomas, 50.
433. Fountain, 113; Scudamore, 118.
434. Dover, 60; Steibelt, 59.
435. Medfield, 2; Manoah, 8.
436. Eternity, 63; Thatcher, 64.
437. Edyfield, 161; Innocents, 138.
438. Olney, 57; Dover, 60.
439. St. Agnes, 7; Barby, 43.
440. St. Thomas, 50; St. Michael, 54.
441. Olney, 57; Bethlehem, 52.
442. Lanesboro, 1; Normanton, 19.
443. Dennis, 58; Schneider, 56.
444. Horton, 165; Wansted, 157.
445. St. Thomas, 50; Bethlehem, 52.
446. Dennis, 58; Dover, 60.
447. Mendon, 97; Chemnitz, 80.
448. Dortmund, 100; Bonn, 101.
449. St. Thomas, 50; Weimar, 65.
450. Christmas, 37; Miles Lane, 25.
451. Edyfield, 161; Weber, 162.
452. Innocents, 138; Monkland, 151.
453. Hursley, 93; Federal St., 91.
454. Weimar, 65; Silver St., 49.
455. Migdol, 87; Creation, 105; Federal St., 91.
456. Manoah, 8; Martyrdom, 14.
457. Weimar, 65; Steibelt, 59.
458. Weimar, 65; Thatcher, 64.
459. Manoah, 8; St. Stephens, 13.
460. Hamburg, 92; Bonn, 101.
461. Hamburg, 92; Dortmund, 100.
462. Barby, 43; Vigils, 5.
463. Dismission, 90; Brengle, 96.
464. Manoah, 8; Bishopthorpe, 9.
465. Invitation, 27; Helle Sonn, 28.
466. Dennis, 58; Thatcher 64.
467. Triumph, 225.
468. St. Thomas, 50; St. Michael, 54.
469. Jerusalem, 22; Manoah, 8.
470. Devotion, 88; Greenfields, 228.
471. Hinton, 221.
472. Stella, 83; Lurman, 85.
473. Palestine, 42; Vigils, 5.
474. Wer Got Vertraut, 136.
475. Vigils, 5; Martyrdom, 14.
476. Sienna, 62; Dover, 60.
477. Old 100th, 86; Hamburg, 92.
478. Manoah, 8; Northampton, 10.
479. Windsor, 26; Trias, 18.
480. Diademata, 71; Olney, 57.
481. Stella, 83; Pollock, 95.
482. Monkland, 151; Oldenberg, 152.
483. Cambridge, 53; Steibelt, 59.
484. Regent Square, 120; Stoerl, 123.
485. Mendon, 97; Duke St., 31.
486. Mendon, 97; Park St., 76.
487. St. Godric, 208; Zebulon, 210.
488. Monkland, 151; Wansted, 157.
489. St. Agnes, 7; Vigils, 5.
490. Manoah, 8; St. Ann's, 11.
491. Regent Square, 120; Benedic Anima, 124.
492. Regent Square, 120; Benedic Anima, 124.
493. Blendon, 79; Truro, 84.
494. Manoah, 8; St. Ann's 11.
495. Steibelt, 59; Dennis, 58.
497. St. Stephens, 13; Knecht, 12.
498. Regent Square, 120; Stoerl, 123.
499. Rosslyn, 230.
500. Weber, 162.
501. Bethlehem, 52; Steibelt, 59.
502. Wiltshire, 29; Barby, 43.
503. Ephrata, 187; Romaine, 184.
504. Stella, 83; Hamburg, 92.
505. Federal St., 91; Stella, 83.
506. College, 160; Pleyel's Hymn, 156.
507. Westlake, 44; Brattle St., 48.
508. Helle Sonn, 28; Eckardtshelm, 39.
509. Abridge, 38; Barby, 43.
510. Silver St., 49; Dover, 60.
511. Cambridge, 53; St. Thomas, 50.
512. Hamburg, 92; Tallis' Evening Hymn, 78.
513. Hursley, 93; Blendon, 79.
514. Chesterfield, 6; Lob Gott, 21.
515. Morning Hymn, 77; Chemnitz, 80.
516. Dix, 169; Nuremburg, 166.

CHORISTER'S REGISTER.—BOOK OF WORSHIP, (NORTH.)

517. Truro, 84; Morning Hymn, 77.
518. Pleyel's Hymn, 156; Oldenberg, 152.
519. Tallis' Evening Hymn, 78; Mendon, 97.
520. Bavaria, 129; Ripley, 130.
521. Penitence, 94; Hursley, 93.
522. Thatcher, 64; Cambridge, 53.
523. Edyfield, 161 ; Weber, 162.
524. Lanesboro, 1; Manoah, 8.
525. Devotion, 88; Greenfields, 228.
526. Mendon, 97; Old 100th, 86.
527. St. Etheldreda, 20; Tiverton, 23.
528. St. Thomas, 50; Sienna, 62.
529. Rathbun, 111 ; Roe, 116.
530. Hursley, 93; Federal St., 91.
531. Redhead, 153; Solitude, 164.
532. Eventide, 215.
533. Weber, 162; Edyfield, 161.
534. Moredon, 41; Manoah, 8.
535. Moredon, 41; Palestine, 42.
536. Ein Feste Burg, 82; Duke St., 81.
537. Zebulon, 210; Old 148th, 207.
538. America, 204.
539. America, 204.
540. Siberia, 112; Stuttgard, 117.
541. Chemnitz, 80; Wareham, 89.
542. Zebulon, 210; Peldon, 209.
543. Wansted, 157; Oldenberg, 152.
544. Herold, 176; Spanish Hymn, 178.
545. Mendon, 97; Ein Feste Burg, 82.
546. Mendon, 97; Duke St., 81.
547. Groton, 222.
548. Old 100th, 86; Federal St., 91.
549. Monkland, 151; Hendon, 155.
550. Abridge, 38; Stockton, 35.
551. Christmas, 37; Wiltshire, 29.
552. Mendelssohn, 173; Spanish Hymn, 178.
553. Barby, 43; Wiltshire, 29.
554. Scotland, 234.
555. Penitence, 94; Hamburg, 92.
556. Anfield, 114; Hollaz, 115.
557. Hinton, 221.
558. Barby, 43; Northampton, 10.
559. Federal St., 91; Penitence, 94.

560. Stella, 83; Wareham, 89; Federal St., 91.
561. Meinhold, 194; Lubeck, 193.
562. Pleyel's Hymn, 156; Vienna, 154.
563. Thatcher, 64; Kane, 70.
564. Duke St., 81; Lurman, 85.
565. Eckardtsheim, 39; Abridge, 38.
566. Stoerl, 123 ; Regent Square, 120.
567. Federal St., 91 ; Hamburg, 92.
568. St. Thomas, 50; Potsdam, 55.
569. Aithlone, 144 ; Meribah, 143.
570. Dover, 60; Weimar, 65.
571. Regent Square, 120; Stoerl, 123.
572. Manoah, 8; Belgrave, 32.
573. Wansted, 157; Innocents, 158.
574. Manoah, 8; St. Agnes, 7.
575. Lanesboro, 1.
576. St. Ann's, 11; Martyrdom, 14.
577. Lob Gott, 21; Jerusalem, 22.
578. Invitation, 27; Wiltshire, 29.
579. Wareham, 89; Dortmund, 100.
580. Hinton, 221; (*omit chorus.*)
581. Herold, 176; Hollingside, 177.
582. Hursley, 93; Federal St., 91.
583. Dwight, 224.
584. Unity, 232.
585. Devotion, 88; Greenfields, 228.
586. Thessalonica, 69; Swabia, 66.
587. Onward, 229; (*with grace notes.*)
588. Weimar, 65; Eternity, 63.
589. Dover, 60; Steibelt, 59.
590. Jerusalem, 22; St. Agnes, 7; Wiltshire, 29.
591. Old 148th, 207; Peldon, 209.
592. St. Agnes, 7; St. Ann's, 11.
593. Mendon, 97; Brengle, 96.
594. Sicilian Hymn, 121.
595. Sicilian Hymn, 121.
596. Thatcher, 64; Olney, 57.
597. Hursley, 93; Old 100th, 86.
598. Roe, 116 ; Anfield, 114; Fountain, 113.
599. Solitude, 164; Innocents, 158; Weber, 162.
600. Stoerl, 123; Sicilian Hymn, 121.
601. Dennis, 58; Monk, 51.

CHORISTER'S REGISTER.
CHURCH BOOK, (GENERAL COUNCIL.)

The Figures in the margin give the number of the Hymns in the Books in regular succession; opposite each of these is the name and number of the Tune or Tunes suited to it.

1. Ein Feste Burg, 82; Mendon, 97; Old 100th, 86.
2. Newcourt, 110.
3. Silver St., 49; Potsdam, 55; Steibelt, 59.
4. Mendon, 97; Blendon, 79.
5. Bedford, 31; Abridge, 38.
6. Mendon, 97; Wells, 99.
7. Duke St., 81; Truro, 84.
8. Lob Gott, 21; Normanton, 19.
9. Elberfeld, 139; Judgment Hymn, 137.
10. Elberfeld, 139; Judgment Hymn, 137.
11. Nun Danket, 213.
12. Culbach, 159; Hendon, 155.
13. Mendelssohn, 173; College, 160.
14. Rathbun, 111; Fountain, 113; Mant, 127.
15. Cruger, 3; Lob Gott, 21; Tiverton, 23.
16. Brattle St., 48; Laucaster, 15.
17. Northampton, 10; Tiverton, 23.
18. Hendon, 155; Monkland, 151.
19. Cantemus Cuncti, Chant No. 62, page 86.
20. Dulce Carmen, 122; Regent Square, 120.
21. Park St., 76; Stella, 83
22. Herold, 176; Tichfield, 175; Hollingside, 177.
23. Stoerl, 123; Benedic Anima, 124.
24. Lob Gott, 21; Medfield, 2.
25. Stoerl, 123; Dulce Carmen, 122.
26. Bortmansky, 167; Nuremburg, 166.
27. Hervey, 40; Moredon, 41.
28. Helle Sonn, 28; Invitation, 27.
29. Horton, 165; Holley, 163.
30. Rathbun, 111; Scudamore, 118; **Fountain, 113.**
31. Ripley, 130; Austria, 125.
32. St. Francis, 36; Cruger, 3.
33. Hallett, 170; Dix, 169.
34. Truro, 84; Hursley, 93.
35. Vigils, 5; Lancsboro, 1; St. Agnes, 7.
36. Dretzel, 192; Meinhold, 194.
37. Hallett, 170; Bortmansky, 167; Herold, 176.
38. Hursley, 93; Nurnberg, 75.
39. St. Agnes, 7; Manoah, 8; St. Ann's; 11.
40. Dix, 169; Nuremburg, 166.
41. Hallett, 170; Bortmansky, 167.
42. St. James, 24; Southwell, 16.
43. Old 148th. 207; Zebulon, 210.
44. Tichfield, 175; Hollingside, 177.
45. Lob Gott, 21.
46. Migdol, 87; Creation, 105; Dortmund, 100.
47. Wareham, 89; Federal St., 91.
48. Horton, 165; Solitude, 164.
49. Brengle, 96; Old 100th, 86.
50. Rudolph, 197.
51. Neander, 131; Allemagne, 132.
52. St. Godric, 208; Zebulon, 210.
53. Helle Sonn, 28; Moredon, 41.
54. Belgrave, 32; Tiverton, 23.
55. Schefler, 109; Ein Feste Burg, 82; (*repeat first two strains.*)
56. St. Agnes, 7; St. Ann's 11.
57. Old 148th, 207; Zebulon, 210.
58. Sicilian Hymn, 121.
59. St. Alphege, 180; Vulpius, 182.
60. Hendon, 155; Edyfield, 161.
61. Anfield, 114; Hollaz, 115.
62. Hursley, 93; Breugle, 95.
63. Solitude, 164; Innocents, 158; Weber, 162.
64. Roe, 116; Anfield, 114; Fountain, 113.
65. Bedford, 31; Lob Gott, 21.
66. Stockton, 35; Lancaster, 15.
67. Wiltshire, 29; Tiverton, 23.
68. Martyrdom, 14; St. James, 24; Lanesboro, L
69. Northampton, 10; Lanesboro, 1.
70. Palestine, 41; Northampton, 10.
71. Pollock, 95; Penitence, 94.
72. Normanton, 19; Helle Sonn, 28.
73. Schneider, 56; Eternity 63.
74. Olney, 57; Cambridge, 53.
75. St. Etheldreda, 20; Wiltshire, 29.
76. Hervey, 40; Tiverton, 23.
77. Wiltshire, 29; Stockton, 35.
78. Rathbun, 111; Fountain, 113.
79. Creation, 105; (*repeating first two strains.*) Truro, 84.
80. Culbach, 159; Monkland, 151.
81. Ilminster, 47; Brattle St., 48.
82. St. Stephens, 13; St. Agnes, 7.
83. Eckardtsheim, 39; St. Agnes, 7.
84. Dover, 60; Potsdam, 55.
85. Carey, 101; Eaton, 106.
86. St. Agnes, 7; Manoah, 8.
87. Tiverton. 23; Lob Gott, 21.
88. Vigils, 5; Abridge, 38.

CHORISTER'S REGISTER.—CHURCH BOOK, (GENERAL COUNCIL.)

89. Southwell, 15; Eckardtsheim, 39.
90. Burlington, 33; Lanesboro, 1.
91. Trias, 18; Belgrave, 32.
92. Hervey, 40; Vigils, 5.
93. Allemagne, 132; Neander, 131.
94. Angelica, 211; Onward, 229.
95. Abridge, 38; Normanton, 19.
96. Diademata, 71; Fairfield, 68.
97. Wareham, 89; Germany, 98.
98. St. Stephens, 13; Normanton, 19.
99. Trias, 18; Hervey, 40.
100. Duke St., 81; Mendon, 97; Blendon, 79.
101. St. Ann's, 11; Lancaster, 15.
102. Steibelt, 59; Weimar, 65; Silver St., 49.
103. Knecht, 12; Lancaster, 15.
104. St. Peter, 31; Northampton, 10.
105. St. Etheldreda, 20; Belgrave, 32.
106. Angels' Song, 46; Lowestoffe, 45.
107. Thessalonica, 69.
108. Mant, 127; Darmstadt, 128; Bavaria, 129.
109. Hamburg, 92; Dortmund, 100.
110. Bethlehem, 52; Sienna, 62.
111. Bonn, 101; Brengle, 96.
112. Ein Feste Burg, 82; *(repeat first two strains.)*
113. Scudamore, 118; Siberia, 112.
114. St. Theodulph, 183; Aurelia, 189.
115. Knecht, 12; Medfield, 2.
116. Ephrata, 187; St. Theodulph, 183.
117. Stobaus, 145; Creation, 105; *(by accomodation.)*
118. Pleyel's Hymn, 156; Horton, 165.
119. Mant, 127.
120. Monkland, 151; College, 160.
121. Layritz, 199.
122. St. Theodulph, 183; Romaine, 184.
123. Southwell, 16; Hawley, 17; Medfield, 2.
124. St. James, 24; Cruger, 3.
125. Rathbun, 111; Fountain, 113.
126. Ripley, 130; Austria, 125.
127. Roe, 116; Rathbun, 111.
128. Mendelssohn, 173; Hendon, 155.
129. Adeste Fideles, 220.
130. St. Alphege, 180; Vulpius, 182.
131. Wells, 99; Chemnitz, 80.
132. Ephrata, 187; St. Theodulph, 183.
133. Ein Feste Burg, 82; Federal St., 91.
134. Christmas, 37; Chesterfield, 6; Hawley, 17.
135. Monk, 51; Olney, 57.
136. Passion, 61; Bethlehem, 52; Steibelt, 59.
137. Ein Feste Burg, 82; Mendon, 97.
138. Wansted, 157; Oldenberg, 152.
139. Herold, 176; Spanish Hymn, 178.
140. Hallett, 170; Dix, 160.
141. Wansted, 157; Horton, 165.
142. Ripley, 130; Mant, 127; Darmstadt, 128.
143. Lubeck, 193; Dretzel, 192.
144. Romaine, 184; Evarts, 190.
145. Winchester, 71; Brengle, 96.
146. Zebulon, 210; Old 148th, 207.
147. Old 148th, 207; Zebulon, 210.
148. Cambridge, 53; Olney, 57.
149. Regent Square, 120; Dulce Carmen, 122.
150. Hamburg, 92; Nurnberg, 75.
151. Helle Sonn, 28; St. Agnes, 7.
152. Hervey, 40; St. Agnes, 7.
153. Trias, 18; St. Agnes, 7.
154. Coronation, 4; Normanton, 19.
155. Thatcher, 64; Passion, 61; Steibelt, 59.
156. Weber, 162; Wansted, 157.
157. Scudamore, 118; Siberia, 112.
158. Dennis, 58; Thatcher, 64.
159. Abridge, 38; St. Francis, 36.
160. Nuremburg, 166; Calvary, 171.
161. Mant, 127; Austria, 125; Departure, 126.
162. Neander, 131; Allemagne, 132.
163. Caswall, 202; Leominster, 201.
164. Christmas, 37; Tiverton, 23.
165. Chesterfield, 6; Medfield, 2.
166. Potsdam, 55; Olney, 57.
167. Lob Gott, 21; Trias, 18.
168. Lentz, 73; Ein Feste Burg, 82.
169. St. Agnes, 7; Barnby, 30.
170. Bavaria, 129; Mant, 127.
171. Roe, 116; Stuttgard, 117.
172. Herold, 176; Spanish Hymn, 178.
173. Refuge, 168; Calvary, 171.
174. Iambic, 119.
175. Stoerl, 123.
176. Crucifix, 188; Missionary Hymn, 191.
177. Herold, 176; Spanish Hymn, 178.
178. Mant, 127.
179. Palestine, 42; Trias, 18.
180. Schneider, 56; Passion, 61.
181. Trias, 18; Palestine, 12.
182. Roe, 116; Hollaz, 115; Bavaria, 129.
183. Winchester, 71; Nurnberg, 75.
184. Hallett, 170; Refuge, 168; Calvary, 171.
185. Konigsberg, 134.
186. Rest, 212.
187. Vigils, 5; Barby, 43.
188. Hamburg, 92; Bonn, 101.
189. Hollaz, 115; Scudamore, 118.
190. Germany, 98; Federal St., 91.
191. Neander, 131; Gounod, 135.
192. Mendelssohn, 173; Hendon, 155.
193. Ephrata, 187; Lausanne, 186.
194. Bohemia, 179; Leipsic, 181.
195. Dretzel, 192; Meinhold, 194.
196. Dretzel, 192; Meinhold, 194.

CHORISTER'S REGISTER.—CHURCH BOOK, (GENERAL COUNCIL.)

197. Miles Lane, 25; Coronation, 4.
198. Bedford, 31; Chesterfield, 6.
199. Ein Feste Burg, 82; Mendon, 97.
200. Mendelssohn, 173; Monkland, 151.
201. Creation, 105; Ein Feste Burg, 82.
202. Abridge, 38; St. Ann's, 11.
203. Vulpius, 182; St. Alphege, 180.
204. St. Ann's, 11; Barby, 43.
205. Miles Lane, 25; Eckardtsheim, 39.
206. Allemagne, 182; Neander, 131.
207. Peldon, 209; Zebulon, 210.
208. Mant, 127.
209. Ein Feste Burg, 82; Park St., 76; Migdol, 87.
210. Zebulon, 210; St. Godric, 208.
211. Peldon, 209; Old 148th, 207.
212. Melita, 108; Eaton, 105.
213. Regent Square, 120; Benedic Anima, 124.
214. St. Theodulph, 183; Ephrata, 187.
215. Coronation, 4; Miles Lane, 25.
216. Medfield, 2.
217. Stockton, 35; Burlington, 33.
218. Peldon, 209; Old 148th, 207.
219. Zebulon, 210; Old 148th, 207.
220. Come, 133; Allemagne, 132.
221. St. Peter, 34; St. Etheldreda, 20.
222. Innocents, 158; Holley, 163; Edyfield, 161.
223. College, 190; Culbach, 159.
224. Lob Gott, 21; Trias, 18.
225. Hervey, 40; Knecht, 12.
226. Dix, 169; Bortnansky, 167.
227. Moredon, 41; Tiverton, 23.
228. Helle Sonn, 28; Wiltshire, 29.
229. Solitude, 144; Weber, 162.
230. Dretzel, 192; Meinhold, 194.
231. Hollingside, 177; Herold, 176; Span. Hy., 178.
232. Nuremburg, 136.
233. Vigils, 5; Windsor, 26.
234. Palestine, 42; St. Agnes, 7.
235. Calkin, 193. Theoctistus, 289.
236. Vienna, 154; Monkland, 151; Edyfield, 161.
237. Thatcher, 64; Passion, 61.
238. Dix, 169; Bortnansky, 167.
239. Scheffler, 109.
240. Resignation, 141; Calm, 140.
241. Thatcher, 64; St. Thomas, 50.
242. Ripley, 130; Darmstadt, 128.
243. Pleyel's Hymn, 156; St. George, 174.
244. Mendon, 97; Lurman, 85.
245. Veni Sanctus Spiritus, 172.
246. Italian Hymn, 203; Olivet, 206.
247. Winchester, 74; Lurman, 85.
248. Germany, 98; Bonn, 101.
249. Morning Star, 146.
250. Lausanne, 186; Missionary Hymn, 191.

251. Mant, 127; Darmstadt, 128.
252. Come, 133; Konigsberg, 134.
253. St. Agnes, 7; Barby, 43.
254. Dover, 60; Weimar, 65.
255. Wareham, 89; Penitence, 94.
256. Wansted, 157; Spanish Hymn, 178.
257. Oldenberg, 152; Pleyel's Hy., 156; Herold, 176
258. Horton, 165; Hollingside, 177.
259. Medfield, 2.
260. St. James, 24; Barnby, 30; Northampton, 10.
261. Olney, 57; Potsdam, 55; Dover, 60.
262. Italian Hymn, 203; America, 204.
263. Bonn, 101; Penitence, 94.
264. Invitation, 27; Lanesboro, 1.
265. Old 148th, 207; Zebulon, 210.
266. Ripley. 130; Darmstadt, 128.
267. Peldon, 209; Old 148th, 207.
268. Adolphus, 142; Meribah, 143.
269. Cambridge, 53; Steibelt, 59.
270. Regent Square, 120; Stoerl, 123.
271. Allemagne, 182; Neander, 131.
272. Iambic, 119.
273. Ilminster, 47; Westlake, 44.
274. Ein Feste Burg, (proper;) 138.
275. Potsdam, 55; Olney, 57; Steibelt, 59.
276. Iambic, 119.
277. Old 148th, 207; St. Godric, 208.
278. Weber, 162; Edyfield, 161.
279. Aithlone, 144; Adolphus, 142.
280. Bedford, 31; Helle Sonn, 28.
281. Helle Sonn, 28; Bedford, 31.
282. Christmas, 37; Abridge, 38.
283. Meribah, 143; Aithlone, 144.
284. Eternity, 63; Thatcher, 64.
285. Thatcher, 64; St. Thomas, 50.
286. Adolphus, 142; Meribah, 143.
287. Penitence, 94; Stella, 83.
288. Dover, 60; Olney, 57.
289. Creation, 105; Scheffler, 109.
290. Scheffler, 109; Creation, 105.
291. Amsterdam, 198.
292. Regent Square, 120; Benedic Anima, 124.
293. Regent Square, 120; Benedic Anima, 124.
294. Monkland, 151; Hendon, 155.
295. Mendon, 97; Chemnitz, 80.
296. Stoerl, 123; Regent Square, 120.
297. Missionary Hymn, 191; St. Theodulph, 183.
298. Monkland, 151; Culbach, 159.
299. Austria, 125; Departure, 126.
300. Lurman, 85; Federal St., 91.
301. Italian Hymn, 203; America, 204.
302. St. Alphege, 180; Vulpius, 182; Miss Hy., 191.
303. St. George, 174; Innocents, 158.
304. Mendelssohn, 173; St. George, 174.

CHORISTER'S REGISTER.—CHURCH BOOK, (GENERAL COUNCIL.)

305. Aurelia, 189; Romaine, 184.
306. Lyons, 218.
307. Wells, 99; Ein Feste Burg, 82.
308. Newcourt, 110.
309. Bishopthorpe, 9; Northampton, 10.
310. Lancsboro, 1.
311. Bishopthorpe, 9; St. Stephens, 13.
312. Normanton, 19; Tiverton, 23.
313. Layritz, 199.
314. Brattle St., 48; Lowestoffe, 45.
315. Lowestoffe, 45.
316. Truro, 84; Mendon, 97.
317. Culbach, 179; Monkland, 151.
318. Rudolph, 197.
319. Resignation, 141.
320. Invitation, 27; Lob Gott, 21.
321. Edyfield, 161; Holley, 163.
322. Mant, 127; Darmstadt, 128.
323. Stoerl, 123.
324. Federal St., 91; Dortmund, 100.
325. Northampton, 10; Invitation, 27.
326. Monkland, 151; Culbach, 159.
327. St. Godric, 208; Old 148th, 207.
328. Martyrdom, 14; Vigils, 5.
329. Dennis, 58; Passion, 61.
330. Old 100th, 86; Germany, 98.
331. Wiltshire, 29; Martyrdom, 14; Normanton, 19.
332. Calm, 140; Resignation, 141.
333. Amsterdam, 198.
334. Bach, 149.
335. Crucifix, 188; Aurelia, 189; Miss. Hy., 191.
336. Hursley, 93; Park St., 76.
337. Redhead, 153; Weber, 162.
338. Blendon, 79; Wareham, 89.
339. Herold, 176; (slur 3d and 2d notes from end of every other strain.)
340. Solitude, 164; Redhead, 153.
341. Lausanne, 186; Aurelia, 189.
342. Leipsic, 181; Bohemia, 179.
343. Old 148th, 207; St. Godric, 208.
344. Normanton, 19; Wiltshire, 29.
345. Wiltshire, 29; Helle Sonn, 28.
346. Steibelt, 59; Thatcher, 64.
347. Weber, 162; Edyfield, 161.
348. Solitude, 164; Edyfield, 161.
349. Come, 133; Konigsberg, 134.
350. Mendon, 97; Dortmund, 100.
351. Redhead, 153; Solitude, 164.
352. Moredon, 41; Manoah, 8.
353. Luneberg, 150.
354. Elberfeld, 139; Judgment Hymn, 137.
355. Penitence, 94; Nurnburg, 75.
356. Penitence, 94; Pollock, 95.
357. Trias, 18; Manoah, 8.

358. Bethlehem, 52; Thatcher, 64; Steibelt, 59.
359. Eaton, 106; Melita, 103.
360. Scheffler, 109.
361. Kane, 70.
362. Swabia, 66; Kane, 70.
363. Lancsboro, 1; Eckardtsheim, 39.
364. Helle Sonn, 28; St. Agnes, 7.
365. Dover, 60; Monk, 51.
366. Blendon, 79; Federal St., 91.
367. Refuge, 168; Hallet, 170; Calvary, 171.
368. Crucifix, 188; Lausanne, 186.
369. St. Francis, 36; Hervey, 40.
370. St. Ann's, 11; Abridge, 38.
371. Hursley, 93; Winchester, 74.
372. Mendon, 97; Ein Feste Burg, 82.
373. Scheffler, 109; Carey, 104.
374. Scheffler, 109; Carey, 104.
375. St. Thomas, 50; St. Michael, 54.
376. Kane, 70; Swabia, 66.
377. Invitation, 27; Martyrdom, 14.
378. St. Michael, 54; Thatcher, 64.
379. Horton, 165; Wansted, 157.
380. Vigils, 5; Manoah, 8.
381. Leoni, 211.
382. Abridge, 38; Normanton, 19.
383. Thatcher, 64; Potsdam, 55.
384. Lob Gott, 21; St. Agnes, 7.
385. Lowestoffe, 45.
386. Olivet, 206; (repeat fifth line of each verse.)
387. St. Thomas, 50; St. Michael, 54.
388. Olney, 57; Eternity, 63.
389. Nurnberg, 75; Wareham, 89.
390. Vienna, 154; Pleyel's Hymn, 156.
391. Vespers, 102; Brengle, 96.
392. Eternity, 63; Dover, 60.
393. Belgrave, 32; Abridge, 38.
394. Monkland, 151; Horton, 165.
395. Hervey, 40; Eckardtsheim, 39.
396. Abridge, 38; Barby, 43; Lancsboro, 1.
397. Belgrave, 32; Vigils, 5.
398. Morning Hymn, 77; Bonn, 101.
399. St. Agnes, 7; Manoah, 8.
400. Vigils, 5; Southwell, 16.
401. Fairfield, 68; Diademata, 71.
402. Swabia, 66; Fairfield, 68.
403. Weber, 162; Solitude, 164.
404. Allemagne, 132; Come, 133.
405. Morning Star, 146.
406. Scheffler, 109; Eaton, 106.
407. Scheffler, 109; Melita, 103.
408. Scheffler, 109; Lambert, 107.
409. Scheffler, 109; Lambert, 107.
410. Hervey, 40; Burlington, 33.
411. Belgrave, 32; Trias, 18.

CHORISTER'S REGISTER.—CHURCH BOOK, (GENERAL COUNCIL.)

412. Brengle, 96; Winchester, 74.
413. Barby, 43; St. Ann's, 11; Lob Gott, 21.
414. Eckardtsheim, 39; Helle Sonn, 28.
415. Knecht, 12; Trias, 18.
416. Bonn, 101; Germany, 98.
417. Burlington, 33; Lanesboro, 1.
418. Stoerl, 123; Benedic Anima, 124.
419. Moredon, 41; Northampton, 10.
420. Belgrave, 32; Hervey, 40.
421. Submission, 203.
422. Wer Gott Vertraut, 136.
423. Herold, 176; Spanish Hymn, 178.
424. St. Theodulph, 183; Lausanne, 186.
425. Schneider, 56; Dennis, 58; Steibelt, 59.
426. Mendon, 97; Dortmund, 100.
427. Steibelt, 59; St. Michael, 54.
428. Zebulon, 210; Old 148th, 207.
429. Herold, 176; Horton, 165; Spanish Hy., 178.
430. Lausanne, 186; Aurelia, 189.
431. Neumark, 108; Lambert, 107.
432. Cambridge, 53; Weimar, 65.
433. Fairfield, 68; Thessalonica, 69.
434. Kane, 70.
435. Olivet, 203; Italian Hymn, 205.
436. Weimar, 65; Cambridge, 53.
437. Hursley, 93; Dismission, 90.
438. Stockton, 35; St. Agnes, 7.
439. Nun Danket, 213.
440. Herold, 176; Tichfield, 175.
441. Lob Gott, 21; Bedford, 31.
442. Thatcher, 64; Dover, 60.
443. Cambridge, 53; St. Thomas, 50; Steibelt, 59.
444. Austria, 125; Departure, 126; Darmstadt, 128.
445. Chemnitz, 80; Blendon, 79.
446. Melita, 103; Eaton, 106.
447. Seelenbrautigam, 217.
448. Luneberg, 150.
449. Old 100th, 86; Lentz, 73.
450. Wareham, 89; Bonn, 101.
451. Siberia, 112; Roe, 116; Fountain, 113.
452. Amsterdam, 198.
453. Aurelia, 189; Lausanne, 186.
454. Lubeck, 193; Dretzel, 192.
455. Leipsic, 181; Bohemia, 179.
456. Angels' Song, 46; Brattle St., 48.
457. Dover, 60; Olney, 57.
458. Christmas, 37; Miles Lane, 25.
459. Chemnitz, 80; Morning Hymn, 77.
460. Migdol, 87; Creation, 105; Federal St., 91.
461. Manoah, 8; Martyrdom, 14.
462. Weimar, 65; Silver St., 49.
463. Weimar, 65; Steibelt, 59.
464. Creation, 105; (*repeat first two strains.*)
465. St. Thomas, 50; Weimar, 65.

466. St. Agnes, 7; Trias, 18.
467. Meribah, 143; Adolphus, 142.
468. Park St., 76; Hursley, 93.
469. Vespers, 102; Tallis' Evening Hymn, 78.
470. Helle Sonn, 28; Windsor, 26.
471. Hallett, 170; Nuremburg, 166.
472. Holley, 163; Spanish Hymn, 178.
473. Solitude, 164; Holley, 163; Pleyel's Hy., 156.
474. Hursley, 93; Migdol, 87; Benevolence, 72.
475. Lanesboro, 1; Eckardtsheim, 39.
476. Weber, 162; Horton, 165.
477. Thatcher, 64; Steibelt, 59; Kane, 70.
478. Wiltshire, 29; Normanton, 19.
479. Barby, 43; Vigils, 5.
480. Dismission, 90; Brengle, 96.
481. St. Etheldreda, 20; Trias, 20.
482. Hamburg, 92; Dismission, 90.
483. Webbe, 219.
484. Resignation, 141; Calm, 140.
485. Sienna, 62; Eternity, 63.
486. Thatcher, 64; Dennis, 58; Fairfield, 68.
487. Weimar, 65; Olney, 57.
488. Dennis, 58; Sienna, 62.
489. Angels' Song, 46; Lowestoffe, 45.
490. St. Francis, 36; Palestine, 41.
491. Lowestoffe, 45; Brattle St., 48.
492. Lowestoffe, 45; Angels' Song, 46.
493. America, 204.
494. Zebulon, 210; Old 148th, 207.
495. Hollaz, 115; Stuttgard, 117; Bavaria, 129.
496. Hamburg, 92; Pollock, 95.
497. Ein Feste Burg, 82; Old 100th, 86.
498. Old 25th, 67; Swabia, 66.
499. Kane, 70; Old 25th, 67.
500. Nun Danket, 213.
501. Monkland, 151; Hendon, 155.
502. Mendon, 97; Chemnitz, 80.
503. Creation, 105; Eaton, 106.
504. Refuge, 168; Hallett, 170.
505. Vulpius, 182; St. Alphege, 180.
506. Bedford, 31; Southwell, 16.
507. Creation, 105.
508. Horton, 165; Edyfield, 161.
509. Weber, 162; Pleyel's Hymn, 156.
510. Morning Hymn, 77; Chemnitz, 80.
511. Allemagne, 132; Neander, 131.
512. Southwell, 16; Bedford, 31.
513. Cambridge, 53; St. Thomas, 50.
514. Trias, 18; Hervey, 40.
515. Redhead, 153; Solitude, 164.
516. St. Thomas, 50; Sienna, 62.
517. Eventide, 215.
518. Innocents, 158; Horton, 165.
519. Belgrave, 32; Trias, 18.

CHORISTER'S REGISTER.—CHURCH BOOK, (GENERAL COUNCIL.)

520. Anatolius, 195.
521. Penitence, 94; Hursley, 93.
522. Tallis' Evening Evening, 78; Mendon, 97.
523. Hursley, 93; Federal St., 91.
524. Devotion, 88; Greenfields, 228.
525. Gounod, 135; Konigsberg, 134.
526. Italian Hymn, 205; America, 204.
527. Ephrata, 187; Romaine, 184.
528. Hallett, 170; Bortmansky, 167.
529. Manoah, 8.
530. Weber, 162; Wansted, 157.
531. Nuremberg, 166.
532. Roe, 116; Siberia, 112.
533. Moredon, 41; Manoah, 8.
534. Palestine, 42; St. Francis, 36. St. Etheldreda, 20.
535. Manoah, 8; Invitation, 27.
536. Bethany, 200; Oxford, 223; (*omit ties.*)
537. Meribah, 143; Adolphus, 142.
538. St. Ann's, 11; Belgrave, 32.
539. Vigils, 5; Martyrdom, 14.
540. Martyrdom, 14; Northampton, 10.
541. Thessalonica, 69; Fairfield, 68.
542. Hinton, 221.
543. Regent Square, 120; Benedic Anima, 124.
544. Neumark, 108; Scheffler, 109.
545. Neumark, 108; Scheffler, 109.
546. Neumark, 108; Scheffler, 109.
547. Judgment Hymn, 137; Elberfeld, 139.
548. Neumark, 108; Scheffler, 109.
549. Scheffler, 109.
550. St. Ann's, 11; Windsor, 26.
551. Melita, 103; Scheffler, 109.
552. Hinton, 221.
553. Trias, 18; St. Peter, 34.

554. Evarts, 190; Crucifix, 188.
555. Stella, 83; Wareham, 89; Federal St., 91.
556. Barby, 43; Northampton, 10.
557. Pleyel's Hymn, 156; Vienna, 154.
558. Weber, 162; Redhead, 153.
559. Calvary, 171.
560. Meinhold, 194; Lubeck, 193.
561. Sienna, 62; Dover, 60; Steibelt, 59.
562. St. Godric, 208; Old 148th, 207.
563. Duke St., 81; Lurman, 85.
564. Jerusalem, 22; Manoah, 8.
565. Judgment Hymn, 137; Elberfeld, 139.
566. Federal St., 91; Hamburg, 92.
567. Barby, 43; St. Agnes, 7.
568. Penitence, 94; Hamburg, 92.
569. Dies Ira, 148.
570. Althlone, 144; Meribah, 143.
571. Windsor, 26; Trias, 18.
572. Thessalonica, 69; Old 25th, 67.
573. Judgment Hymn, 137; Elberfeld, 139.
574. Manoah, 8, Belgrave, 32.
575. Dismission, 90; Federal St., 91.
576. Konigsberg, 134; Gounod, 135.
577. Kane, 70.
578. Paradise, 216.
579. Jerusalem, 22; St. Agnes, 7; Wiltshire, 29.
580. Wachet Auf, 147.
581. Darmstadt, 128; Departure, 126.
582. Hollingside, 177; Tichfield, 175.
583. Leoni, 211.
584. Leoni, 211.
585. Weimar, 65; *Eternity, 63; Steibelt, 59.
586. Aurelia, 189; Lausanne, 186.
587. Ewing, 185; Lausanne, 186.
588. St. Theodulph, 183; Ewing, 185.

www.ingramcontent.com/pod-product-compliance
Lightning Source LLC
Chambersburg PA
CBHW021405230426
43666CB00006B/638